For information on how you can be involved in the ministry of EEBM, you may write to Hank Paulson at one of the following addresses:

EEBM (International
Headquarters)
P.O. Box 198
4700 AD Roosendaal
HOLLAND

EEBM
P.O. Box 1843
Regina, Saskatchewan S4P 3E1
CANADA

EEBM
P.O. Box 73
Walnut Creek,
California 94597
U.S.A.

EEBM
17A St. Michael's Rd.
Aldershot, Hampshire GU12 4JH
ENGLAND

THE PEOPLE COMMUNISM CAN'T CONQUER

BEYOND THE WALL

HANK PAULSON
WITH DON RICHARDSON

Regal
Books
A Division of GL Publications
Ventura, CA U.S.A.

Other good reading:
    Peace Child by Don Richardson
    Lords of the Earth by Don Richardson
    Eternity in Their Hearts by Don Richardson
    No Fear in His Presence by David Dawson, M.D.
    A Distant Grief by F. Kefa Sempangi with Barbara
    R. Thompson

The foreign language copyrights of this book are with Hank Paulson. EEBM. For information regarding translation contact: EEBM, P.O. Box 198, 4700 AD Roosendaal, Holland.

Scripture quotations in this publication are from the *New International Version*, Holy Bible. Copyright © 1978 by New York International Bible Society. Used by permission.

Many names of those involved in Eastern Europe have been changed in this book to protect them and their ongoing ministries.

Published by Regal Books
A Division of GL Publications
Ventura, California 93006
Printed in U.S.A.

Library of Congress Cataloging in Publication Data
Paulson, Hank.
   Beyond the Wall

   1. Paulson, Hank. 2. Evangelists—United States—Biography. 3. Bible—Publication and distribution—Communist countries. 4. Persecution—Communist countries—History—20th century. 5. Communism and Christianity. 6. Communist countries—Church history.
I. Richardson, Don.   II. Title.
BV2372.P38A33   272'.9 [B]   81-4567
ISBN 0-8307-0806-5   AACR2

Contents

Introduction

The startling message of this book is that Eastern European Christians, all logical expectations to the contrary, are flourishing as never before. They are even holding the Communist secret police forces morally at bay in some areas.

How has this tremendous victory occurred? What is the secret of these humble believers who have frustrated communism's direct attempts to erase their witness to the Son of God?

The answer is an incredibly exciting one! Hank Paulson, the man who first brought this manuscript to me for help in writing it, is himself part of the answer. It has been my pleasure to know him and to share with him the telling of this story!

Don Richardson
August 28, 1981

Foreword

The price to kill a single enemy soldier in World War II was $200,000. The price to destroy a life in the Viet Nam War was $500,000. And yet, the average cost of overseas conversion to Christianity, to *save* a soul, is just $654.[1]

Even though we can never put a price tag on the life of an individual, nor on the saving grace of Jesus Christ, these figures should make us stop and think.

There is a war today whose target is people—people whom you will meet in this book. Today great changes are taking place behind the Iron Curtain. In reality, the communist ideology in Eastern Europe is dead and has made place for an aggressive, repressive system. As a result, there is a spiritual vacuum in the hearts of the people. The crucial question is: Who will fill this vacuum? Who will set them free?

It is my prayer that this book will open your eyes to the spiritual battle we are already involved in and the strategic opportunities we are facing, you and I.

Together under His command, we can make a difference.

Hank Paulson

1
Beyond the Wall

I walked along snow-drifted streets of East Berlin in step with Frans. Every few minutes I glanced at his face to bolster my courage. He had passed through that formidable Berlin Wall many times. I was still a 19-year-old novice. Frans paused to study a street sign. It was barely legible under encrusted ice.

"I think the city center is this way," he said, and turned left. "The weather was always clear when I came here before," he added. "Everything looks different now in this drifting snow."

Somewhere in the distance a town clock chimed 11:00 in the morning. The mere reminder of the time of day had a curious effect. In spite of my commitment to this mission my mind instinctively began its own private countdown—anticipating the hour when, our mission completed, Frans and I would return through The Wall to the safety of West Berlin. But then I thought of millions of freedom-loving people—including my fellow Christians in many Communist nations—who must spend their entire lives, through no choice of their own, in fearful lands like this one. In the next moment, as if

my own thoughts about it caused it to materialize—
The Wall loomed unexpectedly on our left!

Frans halted suddenly. "Oh, no!" he exclaimed. "We've been walking parallel to The Wall!" He veered abruptly to the right, looking for another street which would lead us away from The Wall with its barbed wire, land mines, watchful guards and fierce police dogs. Too late!

A police dog saw us and began barking. Then others joined in, a yapping chorus that sent chills down our spines. Out of the corner of my eye I saw a grim-faced guard swing around and raise binoculars to his eyes. He looked as burly as a grizzly bear in his heavy winter coat. Surely, I thought, local residents must pass this close from time to time. Surely the guard will assume we are local residents and ignore us! The next moment, however, we had ample evidence that even local residents dare not walk where we had strayed. The guard with the binoculars shouted a command. Two other guards came out of a command post below The Wall and strode toward us. For a moment I had the awful feeing that Frans and I had entered a world governed by one cardinal rule—only the worst things you can imagine are allowed to happen!

That impression was strengthened when I glanced over my shoulder and saw three other guards approaching rapidly from another direction. "Something is wrong," Frans said quietly. He touched my arm reassuringly and added, "Stay calm and pray!"

Taking a deep breath, I ran my hand down the front of my coat and felt the Christian literature hidden under it. Involuntarily I pressed several books closer to my body, lest their edges show through the fabric of my coat. Meanwhile, second thoughts swarmed like bees in my brain. *They're only books!* the thoughts said, testing every motivation that had given me courage to travel east of The Wall in the first place. *A few guilders' worth of mere paper and ink printed in a language you yourself can scarcely read! Are they really worth going to prison for? Do Eastern European Christians really appreciate Bibles as much as Frans says they do? How can you be sure that Christians behind the Iron Curtain are all that different from the many nominal Christians in free countries who, if their Bibles were confiscated, would hardly notice the loss?*

Thoughts like these had a strange effect. They seemed to make the books under my coat feel suddenly very heavy. I feared that their weight, combined with the fact that my knees were shaking to begin with, might cause me to crumple into the snow right in front of those fast-closing guards!

"Pray!" Frans whispered.

I prayed. With my eyes wide open and my head held high. To bow my head and close my eyes would give us away. And as I prayed, the "second thoughts" retreated. My "first thoughts" returned—with some unexpected allies!

It occurred to me, for example, that the extreme measures communism employs to suppress the Bible simply testify to its profound importance. A book which could arouse such determined opposition from its enemies surely deserved equally determined support from its friends! I decided that, as a believer in biblical truth, I could not abandon our mission. For the moment, whatever trembling remained in my knees seemed due more to the cold than to my fear. I faced the guards surrounding us.

"Passports!" one of them barked, eyeing us suspiciously. Frans held his ready and handed it over. I rummaged for mine. Perhaps this nightmare's cardinal rule had already determined that I would be unable to find it. But I did find it—with a sigh of relief—and held it out. The guard snatched it from my hand and thumbed through it.

"You are too close to The Wall!" he growled in rough German. "Just what are you up to?"

"We thought we were heading downtown," Frans replied casually, but not too casually. Some guards are proud of their ability to instill fear. Showing a little fear, therefore, gratifies their egos. Showing no fear at all may be interpreted as a challenge!

"Could you tell us the best way to go?" Frans added hopefully. But the eyes of the five guards looked as cold as the sights on their automatic rifles.

"Wait here!" the first guard gruffed, and walked away followed by two others. The fourth and fifth stayed to detain us. Minutes passed. Now that we were standing still, a cold wind chilled us to the very marrow of our bones. I recalled a book I read as a boy—a book by C. S. Lewis about a beautiful land cursed with endless winter. Summer never came because endless winter suited a witch who had seized control. A certain immortal lion, however, possessed power to dispel that winter with the warmth of his breath—if only he would appear and breathe upon the snow!

The allegory struck a chord. Suddenly I could appreciate the plight of citizens in Lewis's mythical land in very modern, very non-mythical terms. For there was a sense in which—as in Lewis's novel—it was "always winter" east of The Wall. I smiled to think that the literature hidden under our coats contained "warm breath" from a certain "Immortal Lion"—enough, we hoped, to melt a few more drifts in an icebound land.

For the moment, however, the cold breath of our immediate situation kept Frans and me shifting from one foot to the other. I wanted to jump up and down and swing my arms, but I dared not. The motion might have triggered a veritable rock slide of literature from under my coat!

What would the guards do, I wondered, if they searched us and found the literature? Would they threaten us with their automatic weapons? Subject us to cross-examination? Torture us? Inject truth serum into our veins to make us reveal the names and ad-

dresses of East German Christians? Turn us over to
maniacal brainwashers? Throw us into prison without
trial under false charges? (Conveying Christian literature to Eastern European Christians would hardly
sound—in Western media—like an act worthy of
prison!)

The very thought that even one of these things
might befall us almost unnerved me. Yes, I had considered the possibility before, but only (I realized now) in a
vague, academic way. But there was nothing vague now
about the cold glare in the guards' eyes. Nor was there
anything merely academic in the way they kept their
hands on their automatic weapons.

Just to keep my mind preoccupied, I let my thoughts
drift back to the previous summer, when Frans and I
decided to make this trip together.

Frans, a Dutchman like myself, had traveled widely
in Christian ministry throughout West Germany. I too,
since I committed my life to Christ four years earlier,
had begun to venture beyond the borders of my homeland to minister the gospel. It was so natural when I
met Frans to join forces with him in our common
cause. Buoyant with faith and optimism, we spent a
summer together holding open-air meetings throughout Germany. Our schedule led us eventually to West
Berlin. Then, gradually, Frans began letting me in on a
startling secret—he had been venturing for Christ on
special missions behind the Iron Curtain!

"How exciting!" I responded. "Will you go again
sometime?"

"When God leads the way," he responded. I wondered how Frans would know when God was leading. I
soon found out.

One evening, after a service in a West Berlin church,
a group of people approached Frans with a special request. At first they eyed me, wondering if they should
mention their request in my presence. Frans assured

them I could be trusted.

"We are refugees from East Berlin," they explained. "We fled to freedom here in West Berlin before the Communists built The Wall. We all have Christian relatives and friends remaining in East Berlin. Things are difficult for them. They lack the Bibles and scriptural teaching aids they need to reinforce young believers in the faith, and it is forbidden for them to print such aids in East Germany. Meanwhile, Communist schoolteachers and professors try constantly to brainwash young Christians with atheistic teachings. We want desperately to transport literature to our friends, but our German passports reveal that we were born in East Berlin. It is thus impossible for us to return. That is the reason—"

"You want us to carry the literature, since we carry Dutch passports!" Frans interrupted, glancing sideways at me as he emphasized that little word "us" in a way that made my heartbeat quicken involuntarily.

"Yes," the members of the group responded, almost in unison.

Frans scanned their eager faces. Then he glanced again at me. "My friend and I must pray together about your request," he replied. "We'll give you our answer in the morning."

"Have you ever considered undertaking such a mission?" Frans asked me later.

"No, but I'm willing to go if it is God's will," I said.

"It could be dangerous," Frans warned. "If we are caught carrying the literature, the consequences could be unpleasant."

We prayed together, seeking God's will, and then slept. When we awoke the next morning we looked at each other and knew immediately that we must undertake the mission, no matter what consequences might befall us.

So here we are, I thought, trying to wiggle my numb toes inside my boots. That faraway town clock chimed again. We had been standing there less than half an hour. It seemed twice as long!

Just then a Russian-made jeep rounded a corner, bouncing over ruts in the snow. It skidded to a stop in front of us.

"Get in!" one of the guards ordered. We climbed into the jeep. The guards climbed in after us. A moment later we were speeding down one wintry street after another. By this time I had lost all sense of direction. Finally the jeep stopped in front of an immense building—the Border Police Headquarters.

The guards herded us through a door and down a long corridor. Stopping beside still another door, they ushered us through it. We found ourselves facing an officer with four stars on his shoulder. The guards saluted him. He acknowledged their salute, then took our measure.

"Do you speak German?" he asked.

"Yes," Frans replied.

"And you?" the officer continued, fixing his gaze upon me.

"Only a little," I responded. My voice sounded surprisingly calm, considering the tension within me. *Perhaps I am cut out for this sort of venture after all*, I mused. But in the next moment I chided myself for my secret bravado for, to be quite honest, I was still drawing much of my composure from Frans. *What if the border police decide to interrogate us separately?* I asked myself. *Worse yet, what if they search me and discover that my clothing is mainly literature? How composed will I be then?*

"Who are you?" the officer asked. We hardly had time to answer before he jabbed us with a second question: "Where do you live?" And then a third: "Why are you here?" Followed by a fourth: "What is your profession?"

He really knew how to shoot from the lip.

One thing seemed to be on our side. The building's heating system was either in disrepair or else there was

not enough fuel to keep it running. It was, consequent-
ly, so cold—even inside that office—that our interrogator himself wore a heavy coat! Hopefully, then, it would
not occur to him to invite us to remove our coats.

For nearly an hour, the official rained questions
upon us in staccato German. Often he repeated questions we had already answered, just to see if our answers were consistent. Finally "Take them to Volks Polisci!" he ordered. The guards saluted and led us back
down that long corridor and out into the wind-blown
snow. I wondered gloomily if "Volks Polisci" might turn
out to be some sort of monster to whom suspicious-
looking foreigners were thrown as food.

"Where are they taking us?" I asked Frans, using the
wind as a cover for my voice.

"To *V.O.P.O.*; the People's Police," he responded
grimly. My assessment, I decided, had not been entirely
inaccurate!

Minutes later, the jeep disgorged us again, this time
in front of VOPO's headquarters. Inside, we faced a second official, who promptly barraged us with precisely
the same questions our earlier inquisitor had asked.
Gradually, the sheer monotony of answering so many
simple questions began to irk me. Trying to remove
suspicion from a Communist's mind, I found, is like
trying to sweep dust from a dirt floor. No matter how
much you remove, there is always more to take its
place.

Later Frans explained to me that communism en-
genders monotony, not out of stupidity, but deliberately and with diabolical cleverness! Keen, inquiring
people are more likely to cause problems for the state.
Reduced to a common level of bored inactivity, such
people are less likely to pose a threat. In a few cases, the
boredom itself may provoke them to manifest any latent
hostility against the State. In that event, a Communist
State simply resorts to its second most popular weapon.
Terror.

"You may go," said the official unexpectedly. I cast an inquiring glance at Frans. Did this mean we were free? His expression simply bounced the question back to me. We walked out of that office into a great central hall of the building. Fully armed soldiers stood waiting in ranks.

"Go with the soldiers," one guard said. The soldiers quickly formed a file on each side and marched us outside. An army truck waited, engine running.

Two soldiers jumped into the cabin of the truck. The others escorted us around to the back and said, "Get in!" We climbed into the canvas-covered rear-section and sat facing each other. Frans's face still radiated peace when he glanced at me, but he managed not to look too saint-like when facing the soldiers, 10 of whom now crowded beside us on the two benches. The truck lurched forward.

Actually, I was glad the soldiers were not in a back-slapping mood. One slap on our backs and the slapper might feel the books! I leaned back against the frame-work of the truck just to make sure no one tried!

"Where are you taking us?" Frans asked. The soldiers ignored the question.

Minutes later, the truck stopped beside a well-guarded gate. The 10 soldiers jumped out and waved us after them. Once again they marched us up to the door of a large building. Another guard opened the door. We entered and climbed two flights of stairs. Guards stood at attention on every landing. On the third floor we walked through a maze of corridors. Glancing down one corridor I saw rows of prison cells.

This may be it! I said to myself. *This may be where they intend to search us! How long will it be,* I wondered, *before our parents and friends find out where we are?*

The soldiers ushered us through a door into an office. A distinguished-looking man stood watching us from behind his desk. He wore civilian clothes.

"You are in the headquarters of the criminal police," he explained. I tensed, dreading a command to remove our coats. Instead, the official began asking us the same questions we had already answered several times in earlier interrogations. Then he got to the point: "Your papers are not in order," he said. "Your passports lack a stamp which officials at the border should have added."

He frowned at us, as if we were responsible for the oversight. Impatiently, he grabbed up our passports again and thumbed through them.

"Oh!" he said suddenly, his countenance softening, "I see your passports were issued in 's-Hertogenbosch, Holland! What fond recollections I have of 's-Hertogenbosch! You see, I was there when I was young!" He sat quietly for a few moments, smiling. Frans and I exchanged glances, wondering what happy memory this normally stern-faced official was reliving. (How I thanked God for evidence that human emotions could still surface among these grim men!)

"Well now!" he exclaimed, returning from his reverie. "Let's see what must be done!" He began filling out forms in a brisk manner. Then he added the necessary stamps to our passports.

"Now you're all set," he said with a pleasant grin. "Come!"

He led us out of the room, through the maze of corridors, down the flights of stairs with guards on every landing, and out to the street. There he paused.

"I'm sorry for what happened," he said, handing us our passports. "Enjoy the rest of your stay in Berlin!"

We took our passports. Relief flooded our minds. I recall looking into that official's eyes, wishing I dared ask if his own passport was properly stamped for entry into the kingdom of God. But I thought better of it. Perhaps another time . . . As we walked away, I prayed that one day, by God's grace, we would both meet again in His kingdom!

Heaving sighs of relief, we walked briskly along while Frans regained his bearings. "Are you sorry you came here, Hank?" he asked.

"I admit I was worried," I replied. "But I don't regret a minute of it! Now that it's over I feel about two years older—and wiser!"

"It's really necessary, you know," Frans said, searching my countenance.

"What do you mean?" I asked.

"Hank, until you experience a day like this one, you can never really feel what it is like to live under communism—or any other dictatorship, for that matter. Nor can you understand how desperately Communist lands need the Bible. It is their only hope!"

I nodded, feeling suddenly very experienced—and very honored to have faced difficulties for the sake of believers in East Berlin. A moment later, the town clock—much closer now—chimed five o'clock. I was pleased because this time its booming tones did not set me counting how many hours remained in our mission! Already I was getting over the "countdown syndrome" which afflicts many young Christians on their first journey behind the Iron Curtain. Some are understandably tempted to abandon their missions whenever delays upset the schedule they have set in their own minds for a quick return to freedom.

Apparently, though, I looked a little too pleased about the way I had stood up under pressure. Frans felt obliged to drop me a kindly warning: "Whatever you do, Hank, don't let our deliverance this afternoon make you too confident. Remember, for example, that KGB-trained police along the Russian frontier are far more subtle than the officials we met this afternoon. If this were the Russian frontier instead of East Berlin, they would have interrogated us separately—for a start—to see if our stories conflicted in any way."

I blushed momentarily at my cocksureness. Yet at the same time, Frans's words stirred me like a challenge from God Himself. Perhaps later I would have opportunity to face even Russian border police for the glory of God.

Reaching the downtown area we dined in a restaurant and then bought a map of East Berlin. We left the restaurant and set out in a cold, murky dusk. Occasionally we glanced back to make sure we were not being followed. At length we found the right street, but, "None of these buildings match the description," Frans mused. "That means we will have to ask someone," he added. I tensed. Was it worth the risk?

Frans surveyed the handful of East Berliners around us—a man shoveling snow, off-duty soldiers heading for an evening's relaxation, and then—a stroller who was obviously intoxicated! Frans headed straight for him!

"Let's hope he's sober enough to answer our question," Frans grinned, "but tipsy enough not to remember that we asked him!"

Greeting the man, Frans said, "Sir, can you tell us where Christians meet on this street?" The man swayed as he looked up into Frans's smiling face.

"Chrishtians?" he slurred, "Chrishtians? On thish street? Hmmmm . . ."

He raised an unsteady hand and pointed to a building half a block away. "Try that apartment building, young man," he burped. "I heard 'em singing their Chrishtian songs in there one night. Maybe they're still around—that is, if VOPO didn't get after 'em!"

The man giggled and staggered on his way. Frans winked at me. "Even if he does report us, I doubt that anyone will take him seriously! Let's go!"

We crossed the street and found an entrance to the big apartment building. Striding down one dimly lit hallway after another, we scrutinized nameplates on dozens of doors. All in vain. *Dear God, please guide us!* I prayed. Then we noticed an unmarked door at one end of a hall. Frans turned the doorknob slowly and it opened! It led into still another, narrower hallway. Frans and I entered quietly.

The narrow hallway led to an even narrower flight of stairs. We climbed them, treading as quietly as possible on creaky boards. Halfway up the stairs a telltale sound reached our ears.

"That's hymn-singing if I ever heard it!" I exclaimed, and bounded up the stairs after Frans. By the time we paused outside a door at the top of the stairs, the hymn-singing stopped. Then we heard voices praying.

Frans knocked softly on the door. His eyes glowed with joy at the thought of seeing East German Christians face to face. The door opened just a crack. Someone peered out at us anxiously and asked, "Who are you?"

"We are Christians from Holland," Frans replied. "We bring you greetings from your friends in West Berlin."

The door opened wider and we slipped inside. Some 40 people filled the room. Their faces were dark with apprehension. How could they be sure we were not informers for VOPO?

"My brothers," Frans said softly, "as we climbed the stairs just now, we heard you praying in the name of our Lord Jesus Christ. It is not our intention to interrupt. In fact, if you will permit me, I would like to lead us all in prayer."

Several taut faces nodded in agreement, and Frans began to pray. I must admit that I was so curious to see what effect Frans's prayer might have upon them that I kept my eyes open—just a little! The effect was amazing. One by one the believers exchanged glances as Frans continued praying. Then their strained expressions broke into smiles. No secret policeman could possibly imitate so genuine a prayer! Loving hands reached out and clasped ours in fervent acknowledgement of our unity in Christ. Mingled prayer and praise welled up around us like a fresh-flowing stream.

After praying, Frans delivered greetings from believers in West Berlin. Then he brought a short message from the Word of God. The people listened appreciatively. When Frans finished, a believer named Thomas, with a knowing glance at our bulky coats, said, "Please come home with me for a little while."

Bidding good-bye to the believers we followed Thomas to a nearby station and caught a tram to a distant section of the city. Soon we were safe inside Thomas apartment.

"At last!" Frans sighed, unzippering his oh-so-heavy coat. I followed suit. Together we dropped our coats on Thomas's bed. The bed sagged as if two small but fully packed suitcases had been dropped on it! We began unpacking the literature.

"As I suspected—our friends in West Berlin have sent more than just greetings!" Thomas exclaimed, his eyes shining with gratitude.

"Indeed they have," Frans chimed. "We entrust these volumes to you, Thomas. They are for any who will treasure their message and share it with others."

Thomas nodded. "Not a single copy will be wasted!" I watched as he leaned over and touched the books one by one. He was as pleased as I imagine I would be if I had just been appointed custodian of a set of crown jewels!

"We had to run quite a gauntlet to reach you today," Frans said. He gave Thomas a brief account of the harrowing hours we had spent in the custody of guards, soldiers and policemen.

Thomas's eyes glowed with gratitude. "You could have stayed home in safety, but instead you risked your freedom and maybe more to bring us these," he said, pointing to the literature. "On behalf of all God's people in East Germany, I thank you, Frans and Hank!"

Thomas threw his arms around each of us in turn. "It strengthens us to know that we are not alone in this world."

Thomas smiled. Then he added, "By the way, if you

had reached the apartment at noon, you would not have found us. We now meet only in the evenings. And if you had stood waiting for us to show up, you might have attracted unwelcome attention."

Thomas winked at us and Frans and I winked at each other. God's timing, as usual, was perfect!

Frans settled into a chair and stretched his legs while Thomas brewed a pot of coffee. "Tell me, Thomas," Frans inquired, "did you ever have a chance to escape to West Berlin before they built The Wall?"

"Indeed I did!" he replied at once. "I have a good education, you know. And in the West I could have found a job befitting my training—with fine opportunities for advancement as well! Here, because I am a Christian, I must accept menial work, with no opportunity for promotion."

"Then why didn't you leave, brother Thomas?" I asked.

"I almost did!" he replied. "But each time I packed to leave, I thought of our believers struggling—with one less teacher to encourage them. I thought also of our young people who must endure great pressure from kindergarten to university—if they are even allowed to enter university! Without adequate Bible teaching they may crumble under the pressure. I decided I could not leave them to face the foe unprepared. Then, too, some of us must remain to bear witness before unbelievers here in Eastern Europe. Looking back now I'm glad I stayed! God has given me great joy!"

Thomas's words left us hushed. I tried to imagine myself choosing to live the rest of my days bereft of both political and economic freedom. Even my idealistic 19-year-old mind was not sure it could have matched Thomas's commitment. Especially with an opportunity to escape to freedom dangling before me!

Thomas poured the coffee and our conversation— one of the most moving I have ever known—continued. Never before had I really grasped what the apostle Paul meant when he described all true believers collectively as "the Body." Sitting with Thomas and Frans in a humble East Berlin apartment made that strange biblical metaphor very meaningful! Had Frans and I been Koreans or Tamil believers from India or Yoruba Christians from Nigeria, the fellowship would have been as sweet! For we are all together just what Paul said we are—the Body of Christ on earth, and "members of one another"!

Leaving Thomas just before midnight, we caught the last tram back to The Wall and passed through without incident to West Berlin. How strange the bright lights, the heavy traffic and the nightlife appeared! I looked back at The Wall and thought of Thomas and the others. Did they really exist? And was it really only 14 hours since Frans and I went through The Wall to seek them? It seemed like 14 days!

Later, as I laid my head on a pillow in a well-heated, beautifully furnished West Berlin home, I discovered that part of my heart was still east of The Wall with Thomas and a host of others like him. Perhaps one day I would return.

II
A New Compass-Bearing

For the next three years I thought often of Thomas and the millions of other Christians in Eastern Europe. The idea that I should devote the rest of my life to share their struggle against Communist atheism had not, however, crossed my mind. I had not even conceived of making further journeys such as the one I had made to East Berlin with Frans. And so the possibility of committing myself to an all-out, full-time, wholehearted effort to help those Christians change the *status quo* in Eastern Europe was still beyond the horizon!

God, nevertheless, had already set a new compass-bearing for my life, one that would direct me irresistibly toward that very calling. And, being God, He didn't even trouble to consult me beforehand! I guess I should have known when I committed my destiny into His hands years earlier that I was leaving myself open to the "risk" that He would come up with something unthinkable. Something I would never have predicted. Something that would keep me leaping from one knife-edge of suspense and challenge to another for the rest of my days! Something so surprisingly "right" for me that once I was into it, I would quickly find it impossible to imagine myself doing anything else with satisfaction!

Not that I had been inactive during those three years! Besides spending much of my spare time in Christian work such as evangelism and youth camps, I had laid out a well-plotted course for myself in the world of business. With the help of a $20,000 loan, I was making good headway indeed! God let me go just far enough to see that I really could succeed as a businessman. He let me taste the kind of satisfaction that honesty, common sense, and hard physical effort could bring.

For me, however, those initial pursuits were only a preparation, a discipline, for something still more demanding!

I will never forget the night He showed me my new compass-bearing encoded among some of King Solomon's ancient Proverbs. I had retired to my bedroom for evening devotions. I opened my Bible at Proverbs 23:4 and read: "Do not wear yourself out to get rich; have the wisdom to show restraint."

The words caused an almost electrical spark to jump a gap within my brain. Deep within my spirit, direction-finding gyroscopes began to spin, as if in response to some new setting of my life's compass. Then, like a ship as it changes course in heavy seas, I began making certain adjustments in my thinking, adjustments required by the new compass-bearing!

"Very well, God," I replied naively (I was still unaware of the full implications). "If I am not to pursue my present course what else is going to occupy my time?"

Even as I asked the question, I was reading still more of those divinely inspired Proverbs. Then my gaze settled upon one that said: "Rescue those being led away to death; hold back those staggering toward slaughter" (Prov. 24:11).

Those direction-finding gyroscopes were now spinning at full force. No excuses could alter their angle. Heavy seas or calm, the ship must change direction or else miss its destination!

Once a man told me that, years earlier, he had found himself unexpectedly staring death in the face for a fleeting instant! In that moment, he said, his whole life had flashed before him! It was almost that way with me as I finished reading those verses. Memories of my past life passed before me like a high-speed newsreel: my childhood in a devout Christian Reformed family; uncounted Bible readings and prayer led by my God-fearing father; the shock of his unexpected death days after I left home for boarding school; my gradual drift away from God as a fatherless teenager, then the six months of spiritual struggle that finally brought me back to God. Two years of vocational training following high school. A summer ministering in France and Belgium as a member of an aspiring new mission called Operation Mobilization. That $20,000 loan. The launching of my business. Continued involvement in evangelism and youth camps in Holland. And, finally, those 14 hours with Frans in East Berlin.

I still did not realize that my prior experiences had been a preparation for those 14 hours. And those 14 hours in turn were preparation for a life of partnership with Eastern European Christians who were struggling against atheistc oppression! Communist strategists were plotting the death of their witness, the slaughter of their faith, hope and love.

But God was leading me one step at a time, and this time I only understood that He was calling me into full-time Christian work. I took action.

The first step that God made clear was to sell my business and to enroll at an English Bible School called Capernwray to learn the great truths of the Word of God. At the same time, I devoured biographies of Christian men and women who learned how to apply these spiritual truths effectively in the midst of a hostile world. C. T. Studd and J. Hudson Taylor, among many others, became, as it were, my personal counsellors.

At times I wished God would lead me exactly as He

led them. I wanted to know in advance just what was coming next! Then I realized that of course He must not do so! Their faith had grown only by trusting God in the face of uncertainty. My faith would have to face the same test. Therefore, I too would have to face uncertainties—a special set of them uniquely designed for me!

So be it, God, I prayed (not without a tremble!).

During a Christmas break, I returned from Bible school in England for vacation in Holland. One day I dropped in at a Christian youth center near my home, and guess who I met—Frans!

"Hank!" he shouted. "I thought I'd never find you! Where have you been?"

I told him about my studies at Capernwray. Frans responded, "Hank, I want you to go with me again during your summer break!"

"To East Berlin?" I queried.

"Not this time," he replied. "This time I'm going all the way through Eastern Europe to Russia itself! Our previous venture took only 14 hours, Hank. This trip will take an entire summer!"

"I don't know what to say, Frans," I said, wanting to test every possibility in prayer before acting. "Give me a few hours to wait upon God. I'll let you know this evening."

By evening I had persuaded myself that I was not yet ready in heart, nerve and sinew for so bold a venture so far into the Communist world. I told Frans I was not available. Later I returned to Capernwray for my last semester. Nevertheless, the thought of Frans's proposed journey would not go away. Finally, I knew that I would not be acting simply out of youthful impulse if I accompanied Frans. I wrote a letter to him at once and ran to the mailbox, but before I could mail my letter—

"Haven't you heard?" a passerby said wryly. "Postal workers are on strike throughout England! Better try a carrier pigeon!"

I knew that a postal strike had been pending, but

had it actually taken effect just when I needed to mail such an important letter?

"I'll try telephone or telegraph then," I replied.

"No luck there either," the man grimaced, "unless you can claim a death in the family or some dire emergency! Telephone and telegraph services are reserved only for government business and the like!"

I sighed. Just when I had finally found the courage to say yes and take my next step there was no way I could contact Frans. In fact, the message had to wait until I returned to Holland for the summer. *Surely*, I thought, *Frans will have made other arrangements by now!* But when I finally contacted Frans and mentioned my desire to go with him again behind the Iron Curtain, Frans fairly shouted, "Well, praise God!"

"You mean you haven't found anyone else to take my place?" I asked.

"I tried," he responded, "but no one was willing. So my wife and I and a few others began praying that God would cause you to reconsider. And He has done just that!"

With mounting excitement we gathered Christian literature for our journey. And since we planned to cover about 8,000 miles on rough Eastern European and Russian highways, we made sure Frans's vehicle was in good repair. Then we set out!

Crossing into East Germany, we soon found some of the East German Christians we had contacted earlier. Giving them more literature in German (and leaving greetings for our friend Thomas!) we pressed on into Poland. Once in Poland, we found a secret Bible camp for young Hungarian Christians who had crossed the border for "summer vacation." Invited by the leaders to minister, Frans and I took turns teaching the Bible through interpreters.

Then we continued our journey into Czechoslovakia and Hungary itself. Probing the niches and crannies of both countries, Frans again uncovered literally scores of Christians. I was impressed. If we could find so many devout believers in just a few places, how many more must there be in all of Eastern Europe?

Later I discovered that the rigors of life under communism had developed a remarkably robust witness for Christ among many Eastern European Christians. That witness had, in fact, already brought an incredible flood of new converts into Eastern Europe's evangelical churches. When communism triumphed in Russia in 1917, there were probably few evangelicals in all of Russia and Eastern Europe! Now, however, Russian evangelicals alone placed their number at more than five million! It is my own impression—contrary to popular stereotypes—that committed Christians in Communist Eastern Europe far outnumber their counterparts in rich, carefree, professedly Christian Western Europe!

Many Christians Frans and I met on our Eastern European journey had been persecuted by their own governments for their Christian faith. Their lives, however, radiated an optimism that awed me. Once I was introduced to them, they would take me by the hand, look straight into my eyes, and with compelling sincerity invite me to return and visit them again.

"Perhaps I will," I responded on such occasions. "At least I would like to."

Then followed further contacts in Romania. Finally, the biggest challenge of all faced us—Russia! We prayed constantly as we neared its borders. By the time we approached the Russian guard towers early one morning, we felt confident that God had prepared the way before us.

With the sun rising behind them, the border guard-posts sent long shadows reaching like sinister fingers across the fields as if to probe our vehicle in advance! We drove right up to the base of a tower and climbed out of our vehicle to find ourselves facing several guards. Then a uniformed woman—a tourist agent—stepped forward out of their midst. She took our passports and handed us forms covered inside and out with seemingly innumerable questions. As if the forms themselves contained too few queries she herself kept voicing still more.

Next we exchanged some of our Western currency for Russian rubles. Then we bought gasoline coupons for our journey. And we waited while the woman gave our travel documents a final check. Finally, the guards themselves began inspecting our automobile.

"Remove all your luggage from the car," one of them said. We complied, and they checked everything thoroughly. Then two guards climbed inside our vehicle and examined every corner. By the mercy of God, they found not a single piece of the hidden literature!

"Repack your luggage," he ordered. "You are cleared for travel in Russia!"

Minutes later we were on our way. From the beginning, Russia fascinated me. It seemed like a strange, new world, a world in which one had to be constantly alert. For example, one evening we turned into a campground to spend the night. An attendant showed us to our camping spot and then struck up a conversation. Finally he got into the car and sat beside Frans. "You could help me so much," he said in low, confidential tones. "I like that jacket of yours and I want to buy it." Frans looked down at his new suede jacket. "We can't buy jackets like yours here. Please sell it to me. I have money. Just name your price!"

"Sorry, friend," Frans replied. "It's not for sale."

The attendant turned to me and pleaded, "Tell him to sell it to me! Please!"

"He's made up his mind," I replied.

Then Frans added, "We tourists are forbidden to sell anything we bring into Russia! Selling is illegal."

"But no one will ever know," the man cajoled. "Trust me!"

"This is my only jacket I brought with me," Frans said with finality. "I need it."

The attendant turned and walked away, muttering to himself. Next morning he returned to plead for the jacket again, but Frans stood firm. Later, driving into a nearby city, we saw that very attendant walking along-side the road—wearing a suede jacket almost identical to Frans's.

"Some other tourist must have sold one to him," I observed.

"And perhaps paid a heavy fine for his kindness!" Frans rejoined. "Attendants in campgrounds like this one may double as informers for the secret police. As such, they may tempt tourists to break the law and then report them for selling goods on the 'black market.' The informer may then claim a reward from the authorities! The poor tourist who was moved with pity for the beggar may then end up paying a heavy fine! He might even face a short prison term."

Chills ran down my spine. Later, back in Holland, we learned that two of our closest friends felt a special burden on that very day to pray that God would keep us from danger!

One Saturday we dressed in our most Russian-looking garb, left the campground and drove into a nearby city. We parked our car, wandered through some shops to make sure no one was following us, and then caught a taxi to an address where, according to one of Frans's sources, some Christians lived.

"Which house number do you want?" the taxi driver asked as we approached our destination.

"Never mind," Frans replied in the best Russian he could manage. "This is close enough. From here we can find our way on foot."

We climbed out of the taxi, paid the driver, and waited for him to drive away so that we could head straight for the home of the Christians. He, however, did not drive away, but sat parked, watching us out of the corner of his eye. Just in case he might be watching for an opportunity to report the exact location of foreigners to authorities, we walked on for several blocks ourselves and turned a corner out of his range of sight. Only then did we dare approach our destination—a large, dreary-looking apartment building.

Inside, we climbed to the third floor and walked down a hallway. Looking over our shoulders to make sure no one was following, we pressed the buzzer beside a door. It opened a crack. A short, gray-haired woman peered out at us.

She asked us a question in Russian. Assuming it was probably, "Who are you?" Frans replied: "We are Christians from Holland," using the few Russian words he knew. The woman quickly pulled us inside and closed the door. Then she walked to a window facing another apartment and closed the drapes.

"Did you ask anyone for this address?" she asked, using gestures to help us understand.

"No," we chorused.

"Does anyone know you came here?"

"No," Frans assured her. "We were very careful."

The woman relaxed and smiled. "My name is Helena," she said, and began to chatter happily. We understood little except her sheer enjoyment of Christian fellowship. She opened a door and showed us eight children huddled in another room of the apartment. Helena spoke to one of the boys, and he hurried out of the apartment to summon another believer who could interpret for us.

Meanwhile, Helena opened her Bible and pointed to a verse in Russian. We in turn opened a Dutch Bible and looked up the same verse to discover the particular spiritual truth she wanted to share with us. Then we pointed to a verse in our Dutch Bibles and she looked it up in Russian! It was slow going, but we were amazed how much we could say by letting our Bibles do the talking.

Soon Helena's son returned with a man who could speak German. Helena introduced him. "This is Brother Peter," she explained. Peter began to tell us of the struggles of the unregistered churches in Russia. Midway through his narration, Helena's husband, Ivan, returned from work. We spent another hour talking with him and then he walked us to a tram which could take us back to where our car was parked.

"You are welcome to attend our church service tomorrow," Ivan said as we walked together.

"We would love to," we replied.

"I will meet you under the big clock in the train station. Make it 9:00 in the morning," Ivan sad.

"Wonderful!" Frans exclaimed. "We'll be there."

Next morning, we hid our telltale Western-style rings and watches and dressed again in our most Russian-looking attire. Then we drove again to the city, parked our vehicle, and took a tram to the train station. By the appointed time we were waiting under the big clock. Striding out of nowhere, a big man brushed past us and we heard a soft "follow me."

Peter! We let him move ahead and then followed at a distance to an outside corner of the station. I still found it hard to believe that so many precautions were necessary. At times I felt as if Frans and I were actors rehearsing a fictional script about Christians living under the oppressive reign of some long-dead Nero. But every now and then the roar of traffic, the flash of streetlights, or the sight of a Russian soldier in uniform, shocked me back into sharp-edged realization that it was no script. We were still very much in the twentieth century. And an enemy far more subtle than Nero was never very far away!

"We'll catch a train shortly," Peter said as we stopped beside him.

"As foreigners we are not allowed to buy train tickets without a special permit," Frans objected.

"I've already bought them for you," Peter responded. "I know all about the travel restrictions."

Minutes later Ivan appeared, grinning. Peter explained, "Since you left us last night, Ivan has not slept. He has been crisscrossing the city all night to inform the other Christians where we will meet today."

I gasped! How committed these men were to the cause of Christ! Peter saw the look on my face. He leaned toward me and whispered, "It just wouldn't do, you see, to spread that kind of information by telephone. We meet in a different place every Sunday to make it more difficult for the authorities to trace us. And the word has to be spread person-to-person during the last few hours before a meeting begins. That way, if someone betrays us, the authorities have less time to organize a raid before we scatter again."

We boarded the train. It quickly swept us out of the city. "Aren't most of the Christians in the city itself?" I queried.

"Certainly," Peter replied with a wink. "But so also are most of the secret police! So we meet outside the city."

Suddenly the conductor appeared, checking tickets. Peter said to us in German, "We'll hand him your tickets. Just look out the window and try to avoid speaking while the conductor is near. If he sees that you are foreigners he will ask to see your permits to travel by train."

We followed Peter's instructions. The conductor accepted our four tickets from Peter's hand, checked them, and moved on without a word.

An hour later we stepped off the train and found ourselves in the middle of a quaint Russian village. As Peter and Ivan led us down a muddy road, I soon noticed that we four were not alone. Others who had gotten off the train with us had not scattered in all directions as I expected, but were following us along the same muddy road! My heart leaped with alarm! *A gang of men from the secret police must have boarded the train with us,* I thought.

"We're being followed!" I whispered hoarsely. I was

amazed that a mere novice like me should be first to notice the fact! It's not like Peter, Ivan and Frans to be so inattentive, I said to myself. A moment later, all three turned and smiled at me.

"You didn't think we four are the only ones on that train who are heading for the meeting, did you?" Peter asked with a chuckle.

I blushed and looked over my shoulder. The people following were all smiling very knowingly at us. Relief mingled with embarrassment flooded through me. Just when I thought I would be commended for detecting a maneuver of the secret police, the whole street had to be full of Christians!

Beyond the village a small house stood alone at the edge of a forest. It was surrounded by a six-foot-high wooden fence—an effective "screen" against secret police "binocular sweeps."

We walked through a gate in the fence and found more than two hundred people already gathered in the yard around the little house. I looked around, eager to take the measure of this crowd of undeniably courageous Christians. Somehow, in spite of what I had heard, I expected to see mostly gray-haired men and women leaning on canes. Instead, to my utter amazement, I saw mostly young adults and teenagers. Comparatively few gray heads peppered the crowd.

Soon the crowd began filing into the house. We followed. In the center of a large room stood a tiny wooden table flanked by two benches. The benches were reserved for elderly folk and guests—hence Frans and I were escorted to one of the benches and asked to seat ourselves. We complied. There we sat, feeling conspicuous among a half-dozen little Russian grannies wearing kerchiefs on their heads. Their smiles soon put us at ease.

Most of the crowd remained standing so that a greater number could crowd into the house. Outside, the overflow packed around windows and doors to listen as the meeting began. Inside, the temperature climbed. Perspiration trickled down the back of my neck. But I soon forgot my discomfort as the singing began.

On all sides I saw Russian faces begin to glow with a spirit of worship. I recognized few of their melodies. Sometimes they sang out lustily—their hearts full to the brim with the joy of the Lord. Then, often within the same song, they slowed the beat and crooned softly, almost with a touch of sadness.

Between hymns, various people took turns reading verses of Scripture. I had, of course, heard Christians in many parts of Western Europe read verses of Scripture before, but this time something was noticeably different. These Russian Christians were all reading from the same Bible! By necessity, not by choice! Craning my neck, I looked around. As far as I could tell, there were only two Bibles and one handwritten hymnbook among those 200 Christians! Tears moistened my eyes. Something, I resolved, must be done about this shortage of Bibles in Russia.

Someone motioned to Frans and me, indicating that we should rise to "bring greetings." I stood up first and said, "Christians in the West send their love to you. You are not forgotten. You are an important part of the Body of Christ which is scattered around the world. We are many nationalities and languages, but we are united as one family through Christ, our Head."

As Peter interpreted my words, responsive faces on all sides conveyed deep appreciation. Peter expressed the response of all when he replied, "We are encouraged to know that God has also called so many people to Himself far beyond the borders of our own land, and that those people know about us and love us as we love them."

Next came the most meaningful part of the whole service—testimonies of those who had suffered for their faith. Two young men (one of them was Ivan's own 19-

year-old son) described how the Communist authorities had condemned them to prison. Then Ivan's son explained that he had again been sentenced to two *more* years in a Siberian labor camp! He was present with us only because the authorities had granted him a few days to visit his family and friends before he departed to Siberia.

Years later I was to learn that Ivan's brave son survived his ordeal in Siberia. Not only that, but he maintained a steadfast witness for Christ in the labor camp in spite of all attempts to break his spirit. Even more remarkably, he returned to provide leadership for a number of Russian churches. And what credentials were his! Three years in a Siberian labor camp was a badge commanding great respect among Russian believers. They prefer leaders who have been tested and proved trustworthy!

Next a young woman holding degrees in music and modern languages explained that she had earlier held a coveted position as a high school teacher. One day, however, a member of the secret police noted her presence at a Christian meeting. Next day, the high school principal called her into his office. "You are an excellent teacher," he told her. "You deserve some special privileges. I can offer you a nice apartment. Soon you will receive an increase in salary. There is just one little obstacle which must be removed first. You will have to forget your religious beliefs. To set a proper example for students, we, the builders of the new Communist society, must adhere to atheism."

The principal looked searchingly at the teacher. "Just be wise," he said. "Then everything will be well for you."

The teacher hesitated only for a moment. Then she responded: "I cannot turn my back on Christ."

"So," the young woman said, finishing her story, "I lost my job. I was forced to take a low-paying factory job which no one else wanted."

She stepped back and someone else began to talk. But I kept wondering if she had ever, even for a moment, regretted her decision. I just had to know. So as soon as I had a chance, I asked her.

"Oh, no!" she exclaimed, her face glowing. "I'm glad I made that decision. There is nothing more important than following Christ and living in a close daily relationship with Him!"

The testimonies went on. Finally, Ivan himself began to share. He had spent more than half his life in prison, including long periods in Siberian labor camps.

Ivan and Helena had been warned many times not to teach their children about Christ. "We have religious freedom," the Communist agents boasted. But then followed their fatal definition of "religious freedom": "Religious freedom means everyone must be free to make his own decision about religion when he reaches adulthood. By indoctrinating your children, you are not allowing them to choose religion for themselves!"

How they could choose for or against religion without first hearing it taught was not explained.

Finally one day, after many warnings, "The police broke into our home," Ivan said. "I was taken away in one police car and Helena and the children were pushed into another. I was sent to prison and the children were placed in State boarding schools where atheism would be taught daily."

Ivan was separated from his family for five years that time. But later they were reunited again. And Ivan still teaches his children to love the Lord. Not even the best efforts of Communist agents could keep Ivan's 19-year-old son, for example, from following his father's footsteps.

I began to think about some of the hard questions the Lord was asking me. Measuring my commitment against that of these Christians, I wondered what was actually most important in my life. My career? Material success? If this small house in which we sat was mine, would I put it and myself in jeopardy by allowing Christians to meet here? Would I be so eager to share my faith if it could lead to imprisonment? Were I a parent, would I teach my children the ways of the Lord if I knew that might lead to their being taken from me?

It was not easy to be certain as to how I might react if I were personally tested on these various points. All I knew for sure was that I truly *wanted* to follow Christ and seek His kingdom first. Holding to this basic commitment, I could only trust God to build true stability within me.

Unlike hurried church services in the western world, this Russian meeting lasted a full six hours! When it ended everyone streamed past Frans and me, greeting us personally and giving us the customary Russian kiss.

"You must have some food," the hostess insisted before we left. She brought two bowls of borscht and put them down on the table. We were the only ones to be fed; I felt uncomfortable eating the thin soup our hostess really needed herself.

Just as we finished, the pastor came and pressed 50 rubles into Frans's hand. "For your missionary journey," he said.

Frans and I looked dumbly at the money and then at each other. We knew 50 rubles represented a two-week salary for one of these people.

"We can't accept this," Frans said finally, holding it out to the pastor. "We didn't come expecting anything from you."

"You must use it for your journey," the pastor insisted. "We want to share what we have." All around him, people nodded their agreement. Clearly we would hurt them if we refused their gift. In fact, they considered that sharing with other Christians in every possible way—even materially—was a scriptural *necessity*, not an option!

Later we walked slowly to the train, talking with the

Christians who accompanied us.

"We'll be praying for you every evening," they said. "We'll ask God to bring you back to visit us."

"We'll pray that you can bring some Bibles too," someone added hopefully.

"But if you can't bring Bibles we want you to come anyway!" chimed another.

Their final words still rang in our ears as we settled down for the long train ride back to the city. I knew that my attendance at that meeting had been a divine appointment for me! Through my encounter that day with Russian Christians God had finally revealed His direction for me. I was to return to minister again to the suffering, victorious church of Eastern Europe. I felt truly humbled, knowing that out of their suffering, these people had ministered deeply to *me*.

The church in Eastern Europe has needs to which the church in the West can respond. The church in the West, if it responds to those needs, will in turn be spiritually enriched by the church in the East. What is really lacking, I realized, was a stronger bridge to span the gap between the two different parts of the church.

And I saw clearly now that God wanted me to fit in as part of that stronger span so that a *two-way* traffic in spiritual blessings might freely flow between the two sides of the gap!

III
Birth of a Mission

I boarded the DC-8 and found my assigned seat. Stashing my coat overhead and my briefcase underneath, I sat down.

It's going to be a long night, I thought, as I tried to find room for my long legs in the narrow space between seats. The magic of flying, for me, lay only in its speed, for I found it far less comfortable than taking a European train. And usually far less punctual.

Before long the plane was filled. Attendants closed the doors, and the cumbersome craft wobbled away from the Luxembourg terminal. Soon jet engines swept us down the runway and into the sky. I watched in fascination as a widening section of Europe spread out before us.

I was on my way to America at last! Staring down as a quilt of European farmland gave place to the gray expanse of the Atlantic I reviewed the events which had led to this moment.

Ever since that journey to Russia with Frans, I knew God wanted me to help build a bridge between the suffering church of Eastern Europe and its western counterpart. Only one question remained—how could I accomplish my calling?

My first thought was to offer myself to Frans as a full-time assistant. But Frans didn't need a full-time assistant. Besides, much of his time was spent ministering in the West. I felt sure God wanted me to concentrate on the East.

Then I contacted "Brother Andrew" (a fellow Dutchman renowned for his ministries in Communist countries) but he also had no need for another full-time worker, keeping his full-time team limited to six or seven people at that time.

Finally I turned to Frans for advice. "If God wants you to minister to the church in Eastern Europe," Frans said, "you had better get going. Launch out on your own! If God is leading you, He will provide."

I had supposed God would link me up with some more mature person, or an established mission that would give me the benefit of their experience. But I knew Frans was right—God would provide. So I decided to start by planning a single trip. After that I would see what God had next.

But who would go with me? As I prayed, God reminded me of a young Dutchman named Johan.

Johan agreed to take a trip with me. As we prayed and planned together we found that God had already provided everything we needed. I had a car and we could pay for the trip from my savings.

Johan and I bought a supply of books and Bibles and hid them carefully in my car. Then at Christmas we set out for Hungary. There in a small village we waited in a place where we knew Hungarian Christian youth would shortly gather for a five-day Bible camp. Gather they did, and soon the house was filled with their joyful conversation.

For five days we remained indoors without benefit of exercise or fresh air. No one dared venture outside lest some suspicious passerby notice the extra activity and notify the police. But those five days were filled with prayer, Bible study and worshipful singing before our God. And by the time the fifth day ended we were all bound together in the closest bond of Christian fellowship I had ever known. It was painful to say good-bye to my dear Hungarian brethren.

Yes, the trip had gone well, I thought as I leaned back in my seat on the airplane. It had seemed that God was saying, "This, Hank, is my will for you. You are doing just what I have chosen."

Returning to Holland I sought the Lord about others to become involved with me through prayer and financial support, but also by personal involvement. It was clear that more people would be needed if any impact was to be made in Eastern Europe.

As Brother Andrew was offering Dutch Christians an opportunity to travel and minister in the East, I thought about the friends I had made at Capernwray Bible School and the great source of untapped potential for Eastern Europe I had seen in them. God seemed to show me not to restrict involvement to the Dutch only, but also to allow other nationalities to personally participate. This would not compete with, but rather complement the ministry Andrew had already started.

As I prayed about the next step to take I remembered how several of my friends from Bible school had warmly invited me to visit them in North America. I decided to make those visits and tell them about the vision God had given me.

It was past midnight when the DC-8 landed at New York City's Kennedy Airport—a full six hours behind schedule! Yet even at that late hour the airport was bustling with activity. I joined a stream of travelers filtering slowly through American customs, and eventually (at 4:00 A.M.!) walked out of the terminal, luggage in hand, and climbed into a taxi.

"Someone expecting you?" the cab driver asked as we stopped in front of St. Paul's House, a mission in the heart of the city.

"They were," I said wearily, "about six hours ago!" I paid the driver and walked up to a darkened door. I pressed the doorbell. No one responded. I pressed it again.

The cab driver got out and joined me on the step. He jabbed at the doorbell repeatedly. "Don't work," he said. Then he began to bang on the door. Still nothing happened. "No use," he said. "Everyone's in bed."

I sighed. I was very tired and felt terribly alone. "Is there a YMCA nearby?" I asked.

"Sure. Come along."

A few minutes later I stood in the dim entrance hall of a midtown YMCA, my bag on the floor beside me. "Eight dollars?" I asked, wondering if I had heard right. It seemed like a lot of money for one little room. The sleepy-eyed man behind the desk nodded. I glanced back toward the street, but the cab was gone. Eight dollars it would have to be!

I followed the man's directions to a tiny cubicle of a room—a mere closet with a bed and chair! But no wash basin! Too tired to care, I toppled into bed and closed my eyes, but sleep did not come at once. A thousand new images had to chase one another through my dazed brain before I could fall asleep.

In the morning I made my way back to St. Paul's House. My friend Dave welcomed me with a cup of coffee in the mission kitchen. "Be sure to stop by again on your way back to Europe," he told me warmly. "But call ahead so you won't be left standing outside in the cold!" he added with a grin.

That afternoon, with a three-month-unlimited-travel-pass in hand, I boarded a Greyhound Bus, hoping to fare a little better at my next stop.

Hundreds of snowy miles later I got off the bus in Fort Wayne, Indiana, and dropped a dime in a pay phone. Marc Steiner, a fellow student from Capernwray, was expecting my call. He and his father soon arrived at the station to pick me up.

I began to feel better about my trip to America when the Steiners received me warmly. Mr. Steiner provided me with my first opportunity to share my vision. He was the president of a rather unusual insurance company. All of his 60 employees met with him for chapel every Friday morning. Stunned to hear of such a thing I asked if it was customary for American companies to hold chapel meetings for their employees. Mr. Steiner assured me with a chuckle that it was by no means customary. "And since tomorrow is Friday we want you to tell us all about your ministry in Eastern Europe at our chapel."

On Sunday the Steiners took me with them to a small Mennonite congregation. In the evening service I shared the concern God had given me for Eastern European Christians and my vision to be a part of the bridge between East and West. The people responded, and that church became the first to support what we now call the Eastern European Bible Mission. Their support continues to this day.

The next day the church sent me on my way to Regina, Saskatchewan, where I met Al Young, another fellow student from Capernwray. The weather in Regina was incredibly cold. I tried to shrink down into my usually adequate winter coat. I was grateful for the scarf Al loaned me to wrap around my face. During that night the thermometer plunged to 40 degrees below zero, the point where Fahrenheit and my more familiar centigrade scales register the same. I had thought it was cold during our youth camp in Hungary a few weeks earlier, but this was absolutely brutal!

The next evening Al took me to a midweek meeting in a small country church. Inside the building the radiators hissed a noisy accompaniment to the pastor's welcome.

"I'm afraid there won't be many people here tonight," the pastor said as we waited. He was right! Six people— one lady and her five children—braved the cold, stamp-

ing their feet and clapping their hands as they stepped
inside the door. The offering for the ministry in Eastern
Europe—$6.19.

*I could do much better than this back home in my
business,* I thought wearily as I lay in bed that night.
"Lord, did I misunderstand your guidance?"

"No," the Lord seemed to say to me. "Trust me."

Through a living chain of personal contacts, I moved
from one city to another, sharing my vision in church
after church. From Regina I went to the Canadian west
coast, then down to San Diego, California, and on to
Texas. Finally I returned to New York.

By the end of that year, Americans and Canadians,
along with Europeans, had given enough money to purchase 1,500 books and Bibles and transport them to
Eastern Europe. Al Young agreed to send out a newsletter for me in North America. And I had formed personal
bonds with North American Christians—initial building blocks for that "bridge" to the Eastern European
church.

God had not failed and neither had His people. Nor
had I misunderstood His direction. Having launched
out without organized backing, I had seen God make a
way. The Eastern European Bible Mission was now a reality!

IV
In the Furnace

Al Young—my friend from Regina—and I walked down the street in Vienna and entered an office called "Intourist"—the official Russian travel bureau.

"May I help you?" the lady behind the counter asked pleasantly.

"My friend here is visiting Europe," I replied, indicating Al, "and we would like to visit the Soviet Union. Would that be possible?"

"Of course," the lady said. "You must plan your trip and make reservations before you leave. And apply for a visa, of course."

"Good," I said. "Where may we go in Russia?"

"Anywhere!" she answered. "Here is a map. You will travel on these highways," she pointed at the map with her pencil. "And you may stay in any of these cities."

"You see," I said to Al as we studied the map later, "we have basically only two choices of routes. 'Anywhere' means anywhere these routes go in Russia."

"Surely there are more cities in Russia than this map shows!" he exclaimed, looking at the map.

"Oh, yes. But these are the only ones we may visit," I explained. "These are the only cities with international campgrounds in which foreigners may make reservations. You see, they try to reduce contacts between tourists and individual Russians as much as possible."

After planning our trip with care, we returned to the Intourist office and applied for both reservations and visas.

"It could take as long as two months," I told Al as we returned to our campground in Vienna and settled in for a long wait.

To our surprise, within a mere two weeks everything was in order! With mounting excitement we picked up our reservations and visas. Then we made a final inspection of the secret compartments in our vehicle—secret compartments hiding 150 Bibles! The next morning we traveled into Eastern Europe and stopped to camp for the night near the Russian border.

Before we went to bed we read Daniel 3 together. When King Nebuchadnezzar made a golden image he decreed that everyone must worship it. But Shadrach, Meshach and Abednego refused to bow to the image and were thrown into the furnace. The furnace was heated so hot that the guards who threw the three men in were consumed in the act.

Shadrach, Meshach and Abednego knew God could keep them from being thrown into that furnace. But they also acknowledged that God might allow them to die in the furnace! Then there was a third option—He could preserve them in the midst of the flames!

To Al and me it seemed this passage was God's special message to prepare us for our trip into Russia.

"God will be with us," I said, "no matter what happens."

"Just like He was with those three men," Al agreed. "Whether He delivers us from the furnace or allows it to incinerate us, He is still our God!"

Very early the next morning we broke camp and climbed into the car. We paused to pray together, and then rolled on our way. My thoughts were full of the

Christians I had met two years earlier on the trip with Frans. I was eager to see them again, and it would be a special joy to introduce Al to them.

After about an hour, we arrived at the border. Guards searched us thoroughly, inspecting our luggage, tapping on the walls of the car and checking our papers. Finally they stamped our documents and sent us on our way into a desolate no-man's-land. We knew we were committed. It was too late to turn back. Russian watchtowers loomed ahead, manned by armed guards.

Driving up to the Russian border station, we joined a line of cars waiting before a closed gate. Glancing down the line I noticed that we were the only ones from the West.

Suddenly a big black car whizzed by us. At the gate a guard stepped up to the car and saluted. The driver spoke briefly with him, and then the gate swung open and the car cruised through.

"Must be a ranking party member," I said to Al. "Or an agent of the secret police."

The cars ahead of us moved slowly, one or two at a time. Finally it was our turn. We drove through the gate, glancing up at a watchtower bristling with heavily armed guards. A guard motioned to us to park our car.

I looked over at Al. Then taking a deep breath, I got out of the car. A stocky young woman dressed in an Intourist uniform came toward us. She smiled and welcomed us in perfect German.

I returned her greeting in German. A moment later when I turned to Al and said something in English she looked at me with a shocked expression on her face.

"We were expecting two men from Austria," she said, a hint of accusation in her tone. "With an Austrian vehicle," she added, glancing at the Dutch plates on the car.

"We got our visas and camping reservations while we were in Austria," I explained. "My friend here is visiting

Europe and we wanted to see the Soviet Union too."

She was silent for a moment, clearly doubting my explanation. Then, taking herself in hand, she smiled again. "Well, I'll be glad to help you in any way I can. I am your interpreter."

What a contrast to all the stern-faced, pistol-packing border police! I began to relax. Then just at the moment when I least expected it she asked a critical leading question and I remembered a joke someone had told Al and me a few days earlier. According to the joke, when you meet a Dutch girl she will shake your hand. When you meet an American girl she will ask you for a date. But when you meet a Russian girl she will wire Moscow for further instructions. There was some truth in the joke, and I knew I had better be careful.

Sure enough, during the next hour our interpreter's questions became more and more pointed. I began to wonder how I could take control of the process yet keep her happy and unsuspecting. Finally, like any curious tourist, I began asking questions about Russia and the cities we were scheduled to visit. Like any proud patriot she loved to talk about her country.

"You speak such perfect German," I finally said. "Where did you learn it?"

"Let me help you get your money exchanged," she responded as if she had not heard my question. She became very efficient, leading us quickly through the border-crossing maze. She helped check our papers and reservations, directed us in reporting the currency we carried with us and in listing valuables such as a camera, our watches and rings, and watched intently while we filled out our customs declaration.

Our paperwork finished, the next step was inspection of our baggage and the car. I drove the car over one of the inspection pits and got out, feeling a strange mixture of nervousness and peace. The moment of truth was upon us. One could never tell what would happen. But I knew God was with us.

Two guards went down into the pit to inspect the underside of our car. Meanwhile we unpacked our baggage and camping gear, spreading everything out on a nearby table. A guard began to inspect everything, examining our luggage for false bottoms and opening every package. He shook the canned food to be sure the contents produced no strange sounds.

As I stood waiting I watched a man nearby get into his car to drive off the inspection pit. Though nothing had been found in his car he was so nervous he drove off the track. Several guards had to go to his rescue, lifting the car back on the track.

"All right," the guard told us, coming up out of the pit. "You may move your car now."

I moved the car ahead to the place indicated. Then I got out and stood beside Al, waiting and watching the inspection of the interior of our car. The guards got closer and closer to one of the secret compartments. Suddenly I realized that my jaw was tense and I was clenching and unclenching my fists in my pockets. There was no way I could ease the tension. I could only wait quietly. I began praying wordlessly. I looked at Al and I knew he was praying too.

"I need a screwdriver," one of the inspectors said. "Do you have one?"

I rummaged around in the glove compartment and pulled out the small screwdriver.

"That's a toy," he snorted. "Don't you have a bigger one?"

"No," I said, "that's all I have."

"You travel thousands of miles with only that dinky screwdriver?" he asked.

"Yes."

"Go ask someone for one," he ordered, motioning toward the other cars being inspected.

I looked around. Not a Dutchman or a German in sight. "I can't speak their language," I said.

The inspector barked an order and one of the other

guards went to get a larger screwdriver. When he came back the two men dismantled and inspected our headlights. Then they removed all the body panels from the car and poked through every hollow space with a wire.

Nearby, Eastern European cars moved through the inspection point at a slow but steady pace while the two guards worked over our vehicle in minute detail. Two officials stood watching, along with our interpreter.

The search was almost complete and they had found nothing. I began to breathe a bit more easily.

"Have you checked there yet?" our Intourist interpreter asked suddenly, pointing to where most of the Bibles were hidden!

Sudden alarm jolted me. This could be it!

The guard searched more carefully than ever, an expression of extreme concentration on his face. "Paper!" he exclaimed suddenly. Then, "Biblia!"

From all over the inspection post, guards converged on our car, exclaiming their congratulations to the man who had made the discovery. They grinned at us as if to say, "Aha! We caught you!"

"Where else have you hidden Bibles?" an official asked. But neither Al nor I answered. They soon discovered the remainder of our cache anyway.

Action around our car intensified. Everything which could be taken apart was removed. The engine received a minute inspection for further evidence against us. Even the spare tire became suspect.

In the midst of all the excitement Al and I were led inside.

"May I go to the bathroom?" I heard Al ask as we were pushed into separate rooms.

"No!" I heard an official bark. And then the doors banged between us.

"Strip," the guard ordered. I began to take off my clothes and he inspected each item carefully to be sure there was nothing hidden. Finally he searched me to be sure I had nothing hidden on my body.

After I dressed, the guard hurried me through the hall to another office. "Sit down," he ordered, and I dropped into the nearest chair. Across a large table from me sat two guards and, of course, our "friendly" interpreter.

One of the guards spoke, and then the interpreter repeated the question in German.

I thought I should really have a Dutch interpreter. I could give them a hard time unless they supplied one. But I decided quickly that would only delay things.

Since my trip five years earlier, when Frans and I had been questioned in East Berlin, I had learned to speak German much better. But I still had to think about how to say things. It would be very tiring. On the other hand, I decided to use my lack of fluency as an excuse to take plenty of time to formulate my answers.

"I'm Dutch," I said, looking at the two guards and the interpreter. "I don't speak German too well. So I cannot be responsible for the exact meaning of any answers I give in German."

The interpreter smiled at me coolly and put a large piece of paper in front of me. "Write your answers," she said. Instantly, I knew whatever I wrote could be used as a written confession.

The questions got under way. I wrote my answers thoughtfully, all the time asking the Lord to guide me. I began to realize that writing offered a further advantage. I could take time to word my responses in such a way that I avoided giving the officials any important information.

"How many Bibles did you bring?" they began.

"There may be 100," I answered. "Maybe 200."

"When you went to the store how many did you buy?"

"A hundred. Maybe 200. Count them and see."

"Who bought the Bibles for you?" they asked.

"Who did you pay for them? How much did they cost?"

"How many did you say there were?"

The questions went on, returning often to the question of number. They weren't happy with my inexact answer. But I felt God wanted me to answer in this way.

In another office, Al was undergoing the same kind of questioning, but with an English-speaking interpreter. All day long he too refused to give a specific number for the Bibles.

The questions went on. "How many Bibles did you buy?"

"Who made the hiding places in your car? Whose car is it?"

"How many Bibles did you actually conceal?"

"Who told you to do this? Who is paying you?"

"No one paid us," I answered. "We chose to do it."

"Ridiculous!" one of the guards sneered. "Who paid you?"

Then they held up a picture of Al's fiancée. "Who is this? Do you know her?"

"That's Al's picture," I said. "It's his fiancée. He knows her much better than I do. Ask him."

"What more is she? Did she send you? How much is she paying you?"

I realized that from their viewpoint only a monetary reward or heavy pressure could motivate anyone to take the risks Al and I were taking.

Another round of questioning began. "What is your occupation? Where do you work? How much money do you make?"

"How much did you pay for your car?"

"Give us a list of your relatives. What do they do?"

"Have you ever been to the Soviet Union before? Where did you visit?"

All day long the questions came, many of them repeated over and over again. But no accusations were leveled at me. I began to realize that they hoped to make me so tired and confused that I would give something away on my own. It was time to declare my innocence.

"I have done nothing criminal," I said. "The Bibles you found in my car are identical to Bibles approved by the Soviet government. True, I did not declare them for customs. Perhaps a fine would be in order for that. But I have done nothing criminal."

Suddenly the pressure increased. With my declaration of innocence they decided to press me for a confession. But God strengthened me. I remained calm and stayed on the offensive.

"Isn't it true," I asked, "that the Soviet government censors literature to be sure the people read only good things? The Bible has passed Soviet censorship. Some Bibles are printed right here in Russia. It is good material by your own government's standards."

I stopped and looked at them. They stared warily back at me, waiting. I went on. "The Bibles I had in the car are photocopies taken from Bibles printed right here in the Soviet Union. They say 'Printed in Moscow' in the front. Every single page is a photocopy. Not one letter has been changed. So the Bibles I brought with me are good, are they not?"

The guards talked quickly among themselves. They didn't want to give the logical answer to my question. Nor did they like being cornered.

"We will ask the questions here," one of them retorted.

As the day wore on, the guards changed shifts, but our ordeal by interrogation continued without a pause. Neither Al nor I was allowed to eat or even to have a drink of water. But through it all, we were conscious that God was standing by us just as He stood beside Shadrach, Meshach, and Abednego right inside the fiery furnace.

"Why aren't you afraid?" one of the guards finally asked me.

I stopped, dumbfounded. He was right. I was not

afraid. I felt calm and I was thinking clearly. I smiled to myself, realizing that the guards were actually more nervous than I. *Thank you, Lord!* I said silently. I knew He was working in me.

I turned to the guard. "I have committed no crime," I answered. "I have nothing to hide. I'm here of my own choosing to show love to my brothers and sisters in Christ. Jesus Christ is right here with me."

"What would God have done to you if you hadn't made this trip?" the guard asked. And I realized once again that they, with their sterile police state mentality, could only imagine we had been coerced by some higher power. If it wasn't a threatening human who compelled us, then it must be a threatening God.

"Do you read the Bible?" they went on, changing their approach.

"Yes."

"Do you memorize the Bible?" They must have heard that Russian Christians claimed to memorize extensive portions of the Bible because they didn't have a copy to read.

"Yes," I said. "I have memorized a few verses."

"Can you prove it?"

I thought quickly. Here was a chance to let God speak through His own word. "For God so loved the world that he gave his one and only Son," I quoted. And I went on to repeat several other verses which gave God's plan of salvation.

"What church are you from?"

I knew that if I said Baptist they would think I planned to visit Baptist Christians in Russia. Or if I said Orthodox or Pentecostal, those Christians might come under special surveillance. "I belong to an independent Bible-believing church," I answered.

"What!" they exclaimed, looking at each other to see if any among them had ever heard of such an oddity before. This was something outside a structure they could understand. "What denomination did you say?"

"The denomination isn't important," I answered. "What *is* important is believing that Jesus Christ is the Son of God and we can know Him personally."

Their questions continued along the same lines. Were they sincerely curious about my faith? Or were they simply to keep me talking until I eventually let something strategic slip?

"I hear that in the West some churches feature rock music in their services," one of the interrogators said.

I thought immediately of the Jesus People movement. "Yes," I said. "Many young people have come to know the Lord Jesus. They express their faith with guitars, not just with organs in huge cathedrals."

"Here in our country, religion is only for the old," the guard sneered. "Do western young people really believe in Jesus?"

I nodded. "Many young people are disillusioned with materialistic goals. They are turning to Jesus Christ for meaning and peace and love."

Late that night a guard finally led me to another room. Al was already there. Searching his face I saw reflected on it the same settled peace which I had sensed all day.

Nine guards surrounded us. Our two interpreters joined them.

"We have a statement for you to sign," the interpreter said.

"What is it?" I asked, looking at the strange Russian characters.

"There is one statement that you have been treated well at the border, and another that your car and the literature have been confiscated."

"But I can't read this," I protested. "Give me a translation to sign."

"That is impossible," said one of the guards quickly. "You must sign the statement as it is."

"But I can't say that we have been treated well," I protested. "Even though the questions were asked in a civilized manner, I consider the confiscation of my car to be bad treatment."

The men began to talk quickly among themselves, their faces growing red. "If you don't sign this statement immediately," their leader said, "you will stay here—much, much longer."

"Do we have a choice?" I asked.

"No."

"Are you going to force us to sign?"

Again the rapid conversation among the men. The atmosphere in the room tensed. "Sign now," one of the men said. "Make your complaints afterward."

"Why not let him write his own statement and sign it?" another man suggested wearily.

It was agreed, and I sat down to write carefully in German. I composed a statement I hoped would satisfy them and which I could sign in good conscience. "Now," I said, "I must have a statement from you for my government explaining why my car was confiscated."

I glanced over at Al. He didn't know everything that was going on because he didn't understand German. But I could not explain to him now.

The nine angry men discussed the latest development in tightly controlled voices. The chief officer's face was red, veins bulging at his temples.

"This is highly irregular," he said coldly. "Get them out!"

Al and I were led to a bench outside. Sitting there side by side, we talked only briefly. Guards stood nearby watching us and anyone could be listening at the window right behind us. I looked at my watch. It was eleven at night. It had been a very long day, and it wasn't over yet.

Inside, the officials' discussion grew louder and louder until we could hear the men shouting at one another. Obviously the solution to the problem I had presented was not so simple. Finally they became quiet again, and we were called back into the room.

The nine guards sat around the table, a smile on every face.

"You are very young," the chief official said in a fatherly tone. "And since you have not been in the Soviet Union before (*why did he say that? He knew I had been here before!*), and you did not intend to do anything against the Soviet Union, we have changed our minds. We will draft a new statement for you to sign. We will confiscate only the literature. You may have your car back."

They prepared the statement immediately. I glanced over it, noticing that only 126 Bibles had been confiscated. I knew they had found all 150 of them. The other 24, I thought, would find their way through the guards' pockets to the black market. Smiling inwardly, I signed the statement.

We went back to the car and began repacking our camping gear and luggage. All around us the atmosphere had changed to one of casual joviality.

I was about to get into the car to drive away when one of the guards sidled close to me. Taking off his hat so as to look less official, he tucked it under his arm. Then he said, with a confidential wink, "Tell me, now that everything is over, just how many Bibles did you have?"

"It might have been 100," I answered as before. "Maybe 200."

I got into the car realizing suddenly that everything could have been reversed at that very instant if I had given a different answer. A little chill shuddered its way down my spine.

It was just past midnight. The border station beyond the no-man's-land had long since closed down for the night. But in response to a phone call from the Soviet side, it quickly came to life. I put the car in gear and stepped on the accelerator. We were leaving Russia.

"The 24 Bibles they did not list will almost certainly find their way into Christian hands," I said softly to Al.

"Who knows, perhaps all of them will end up in Christian hands. The guards surely must know that Christians will pay up to two months' wages for a Bible. It will be a great temptation for the guards to sell them."

Al smiled and sighed. "God delivered us through the fiery furnace," he said quietly.

I nodded. I was glad I had spent the day in the furnace to have experienced God's presence and help. Also I now would be better equipped to train and prepare other teams to go behind Communist boundaries. I could speak from experience.

V
Encounter with Ferri

We inched forward in a line of cars at the Romanian border. I had never felt so nervous in all my life. I glanced at the three girls traveling with me. The one beside me in the front seat looked as if she might faint at any moment.

This was my first experience in attempting a crossing with a group of young North American summer workers, and I felt keenly my responsibility for their safety.

I thought of Al, wondering how he and the other four summer workers were doing. They had crossed the border earlier with a load of 500 Bibles and books. We would meet them inside Romania.

At last it was our turn to drive through the gate and park in front of one of the border office buildings.

"Have your passports ready," I told the girls as we got out of the car. I turned to look at them. "None of you look quite like happy tourists," I remarked.

"Neither do you," commented one of the girls.

I sighed. It was only a few weeks since Al and I had been detained at the Russian border with our load of Bibles. I felt more nervous now than I ever imagined I would. Besides, I was in this strange combination with three girls. We hardly looked like conventional tourists. And we had 600 Bibles in the car!

We waited in the hot sun as minutes ticked slowly by.

"Look!" one of the girls said when a guard beckoned a car behind us to pull out and go around us. "Why have they singled out our car to remain here?" she asked.

I clenched and unclenched the steering wheel. Could the Russians have notified these Romanian officials of Al's and my detention at the Russian border? If so the Romanians might be more harsh with us for making a second attempt.

Still another car pulled around us and drove across the border. No one breathed a word, but I knew the girls were wondering, just as I was, why we had to wait so long.

When a guard waved a third car past us heading into Romania, a cold sweat began to break out on my face. I pulled out my handkerchief to mop my brow.

Suddenly an official approached us from behind. "What are you waiting for?" he asked. "Haven't your passports been returned to you yet?"

"No," I said. "No one even asked for them. They haven't been taken into the office yet.

"Oh," the man said, clearly irritated. "Someone has slipped up. Let me have them."

He took our four sets of passports in his hands and hurried into the office. In a few minutes he was back. "Here," he said, handing me the lot. "Now open the trunk of your car."

I opened the trunk and he glanced inside.

"Good," he said. "Now hurry along. You're blocking traffic."

I stood still for an instant, stunned by the suddenness of it all. Then I said, "Let's go!" and we jumped into the car. We were on our way into Romania without so much as a proper inspection of our car! In time the 600

Bibles were distributed and we returned without incident to Holland.

With each new experience in border crossing I was learning how to handle the stress with less fraying of my nerves. The next summer a total of five North Americans joined me in Holland for our new mission's first fully organized Summer Missionary Program. They were full of anticipation and their excitement had mounted as we prepared for a trip into Romania. This time we had no less than 800 Bibles and other books hidden in our vehicle; hence we could not have been more relieved when we crossed the border without incident. We traveled on, eager to distribute the Bibles and join a secret youth camp.

As the six of us traveled deeper into northwestern Romania, I gave the team members some background on that part of the country. "This section of Romania once belonged to Hungary," I said. "Between two and three million Hungarian-speaking people still live here. That's why our Bibles are Hungarian. The youth camp will be in Hungarian too."

We drove into a certain city and parked to await our rendezvous with Hungarian Christians. I looked at my watch. Three o'clock. "It's time!" I exclaimed.

We got out of the car and scattered through the square. I walked along watching for the people I was to meet. But by 3:30, they still had not appeared.

I wandered around the square with one of the team members as long as I could without attracting attention. Then I looked across the square at an open-air cafe on the other side. "Let's go over there and have some coffee," I said.

"Good," replied my partner. "I'm thirsty."

We crossed the square and sat down at a little table on the sidewalk. Slowly we sipped our coffee, still watching for our contacts. Minutes turned into hours. An aching knot of disappointment hardened in the pit of my stomach.

"I think we should go," I finally said at six o'clock. "Something must have gone wrong."

Dejected, we walked back to the car. I sat in the driver's seat, my hands on the steering wheel, not knowing what to do. The other team members were quiet, waiting for me to speak.

"Well, let's go," I finally said, turning the key in the ignition. "Let's get out of the city."

"What will we do?" someone asked.

"I don't know."

We drove along the highway for about a half hour. Everyone was quiet. I was too disappointed to think clearly about what we should do. Nor did I have a contingency plan ready.

"Why don't we find a place to camp for the night?" someone suggested.

"Look, there's a little road on the left," someone else said. "We could look for a camping spot back there."

"Yes, let's do!" several voices chorused.

I turned into the side road and we bounced along the narrow asphalt until it turned to gravel. Driving on slowly, we passed through a quaint village where the front doors of the houses opened right onto the road. Later even the gravel road ended. Before us lay a grassy open space surrounded by forest.

"This looks isolated enough!" someone exclaimed, jumping out of the car. But just then a train rumbled by! The track was barely 100 feet from us, beyond some trees.

"Looks like we'll have to make do," I said. "It will soon be dark." Quickly we unloaded our camping gear and set up our tents.

I knew several pastors and other Christians in Romania, and I knew we could deliver Bibles to them. But by the next morning I was still unable to settle on exactly how or where to start.

"I'm too depressed to be helpful to anyone," I admitted as we broke camp after breakfast. "Let's take some time for a little service of our own before we go on."

We sat down in a circle on the grass. Our camping gear was strewn around us and the forest was our background. We began to sing.

While we sang, I glanced down the gravel road which had led us to this spot. A man was walking along the road toward us. He looked at us curiously, then walked right by us toward the forest.

We finished a song and began to sing another, "How Great Thou Art," a song of worship familiar around the world. I sang along in English as well as I could, thinking how appropriate the hymn was for our country setting.

Suddenly the man who had been walking toward the forest stopped. He stood very still for a moment, then turned facing us and sat down on the ground. By the third verse he got up and began to walk slowly toward us. We sang on, ignoring him. I knew that as Westerners we could sing openly without danger, no matter what the song might be.

At the end of the song I picked up my Bible. Suddenly the man stepped up close to us.

"*Biblia!* he exclaimed, his face lighting up as he pointed at my Bible. "Christians?" He looked around the circle.

I stood up and held out a welcoming hand. Quickly we sorted through languages until we found that we could both speak German.

"My name is Daniel," he told me. "I heard that song when I was walking by. We sing it in our language too!"

I turned to translate for my English-speaking companions. And then Daniel went on.

"I'm staying with friends in the village up the road. I'm from the city, just here for the weekend," he said. "This morning I felt such a need to go for a walk, to be alone with God. And you were singing that song!"

I translated again for the team members. "That's

wonderful!" they exclaimed.

"Come along to church with me!" Daniel urged. Quickly we packed our camping gear into the car and climbed in ourselves. Daniel got in with us and directed us back along the gravel road to the village we had just passed the night before. He took us to a small Baptist church.

We walked into the crowded sanctuary. Two hundred or more people were squeezed into the room, women on one side of the aisle and men on the other. In front, spilling down into the pews, a brass band of 60 or 70 people played their trumpets, trombones, and even a huge drum!

When Daniel introduced us, the congregation welcomed us warmly. We sang and I gave a greeting with Daniel interpreting from German to the language of the people. Daniel, we learned later, *was the only person in the village who spoke German fluently.* Surely the Lord had brought us together so we could minister to this congregation!

At noon the service ended. We split into three pairs and were taken to three different church leaders' homes for the customary Romanian Sunday dinner.

"You are the first visitors ever to come to our church from the West," our host told us as we ate. "It is so good to know that you in the West care about us and pray for us. We often feel very much alone under the heel of oppressors."

We talked and ate, then talked some more. My feelings of discouragement were forgotten!

At 1:30 we walked slowly through the village back to the church. The service was to resume at 2:00 but when we arrived most of the people were already there, singing as they awaited our return.

A few minutes before five o'clock, the service was still going strong when one of the church leaders leaned over to speak to me. "We must leave now," he said. "I will take you to another church."

Following the man outside we all got into our car. He directed us to another Baptist church in a village not far away. It too was crammed with worshipers.

Once again our team sang and shared with the congregation. "You are part of the worldwide Body of Christ," I told them as I had already told many other Eastern European Christians. "Your brothers and sisters in Holland, North America and many other places care about you."

"This is the first time anyone has come from the West to visit us," we were told again. "Now we know we are not really alone!"

After the service the pastor of that church took all six of us to his home. Soon Christian leaders from the area began to join us, and we shared informally with one another far into the night. Finally, long after midnight, people began to leave reluctantly.

"Come," the pastor said when everyone was gone, "I'll take you to a home where you may spend the night."

"Wait," I said. "That will be dangerous for you because you will have to report having us here. We could just find a camping spot for the night."

"No, don't worry," the pastor smiled, leading us to a little house.

The hostess opened the door, and seeing my worried expression, she smiled. "There are no police in this village," she said. "We won't have to tell anyone."

We fell gratefully into our beds, but there were only a few hours for sleep. Early in the morning we got up to head off again.

"What a day!" one of the team members exclaimed as we drove along. "Hank, you aren't depressed anymore, are you?"

I laughed joyfully. "Isn't it wonderful how God planned it all!" I said. "Let's get busy now distributing these Bibles."

"Why didn't we give some out yesterday?" someone asked. "I didn't see many Bibles in either of the churches."

"Because we were always surrounded by people," I answered. "The more people who know we have Bibles the more chance there is that the police will find out. Besides," I added, "there are sometimes informers among the Christians. We must be very careful to whom we choose to give Bibles."

During the following week, we made several contacts and distributed about 200 of the Bibles. But 600 still remained to be passed out, and we had only one day left on our visas by Saturday. We prayed together that God would let us know what to do with the remaining stock.

"What about Zoltan?" one of the team members asked, naming a man we had met the Sunday before.

"Doesn't he lead a musical group that visits different churches?" asked someone else.

"Maybe he could distribute Bibles when he visits churches," added a third.

"Yes," I said. "I was thinking of Zoltan too. I believe God has reminded us of him."

Late that afternoon we set up camp where we planned to spend the night. Then leaving three of the team at camp, the rest of us went in search of the address Zoltan had given me.

It was almost 10:00 when we arrived at the village. Leaving the car at the edge of the village, we set out on foot to search for the street.

The village was dark and quiet. Most people had already gone to bed. The crack of light under a few doors and an occasional lamp behind shuttered windows were the only indications of life.

Finally we found the street and began to search for the house. Houses in Romanian villages are often numbered in the sequence in which they were built, so there was nothing to do but check every house until we found the right one.

At last we found it and I knocked on the door. An old lady answered. When I asked for Zoltan, she shook her head blankly. Her husband joined her at the door, but neither of them could speak any of the languages we spoke. They invited us inside, and we tried to communicate. Finally by drawing little pictures, gesturing and pointing at words in the dictionary, we managed to inform the old couple that we were looking for their son.

"Which son?" the old woman wondered. I heaved a big sigh and tried to describe Zoltan and what he did. Finally the woman understood and told us he was in the city. Eventually we persuaded her to go with us to the city to find Zoltan.

We walked to the edge of the village and got into the car. After a long drive to the city the old woman directed us through the streets to her son's house.

Zoltan welcomed us warmly. His wife immediately began setting out the customary meal for guests, though it was late at night.

"This is my father-in-law, Ferri," Zoltan said, introducing us to an older man in Zoltan's home. "He is a leader in the church, a very active Christian."

Ferri told us about his job with the government, a job which required him to travel widely in Eastern Europe. "The government provides a car for me," he said.

I could hardly contain my excitement. Ferri appeared to be a very special man. He had a strong, bold personality, yet I saw that he was very gentle and loving toward others. Further, he was renowned for his strong Christian testimony and leadership among the churches. Still more strategically, he worked for the government, something few Christians were allowed to do in Communist countries. And he had a car in a land where there were usually no more than one or two cars per village.

"Ferri," I finally said, trying to control the excitement in my voice, "could you distribute some Bibles?"

"Yes, of course!" he exclaimed.

"Could you distribute quite a few?"

"Yes, I'd love to," he said, his eyes filling with questions.

"We have about 600 Bibles and books," I said. "Could you use them?"

Tears began to run down Ferri's cheeks. "Wh—what language are they in?" he finally managed to choke out.

"Hungarian," I said. "I'm sorry we have no Romanian ones right now."

Ferrie continued to cry. I waited silently, wondering just what was going on inside him.

"Hungarian Bibles are exactly what we need right now," he finally managed to say. "More than anything else."

"Well, praise the Lord!" I exclaimed softly, as tears of joy moistened my own eyes.

Soon we left, taking Zoltan's mother back to her home. We delivered the 600 Bibles to Ferri that same night. We also talked with him about possible future contacts.

Later the same summer we were able to provide Ferri with some Romanian Bibles as well. Since then he has become a strategic contact for us, carrying a few Bibles with him on every trip he makes around the country for the government.

It was early morning by the time we got back to camp. Excitedly, we reported to the rest of the team how God had led us to the ideal person to distribute the Bibles.

"And the government is even helping him to do it!" someone exclaimed.

"We can be thankful the youth camp didn't work out!" a second said.

"Commit your way to the Lord," I quoted as the verse came to my mind; "trust in him and he will do this" (Ps. 37:5).

We knelt together and thanked God for leading us in His way and showing us His care once again.

VI
Communism: Does It Really Work?

"Students, can anyone tell me the names of the first people on earth?"

"Adam and Eve, Comrade Teacher," said young Ivan.

"Good, Ivan. And where did they live?"

"They must have lived in Russia," Ivan replied.

"Why do you think they lived in Russia?" the teacher asked in surprise.

"Simple, Comrade Teacher," Ivan replied. "They had no house, no clothes, and they had to forage food from the trees. And yet they called it paradise!"

With some exaggeration, this describes the reality of Communist countries where millions have precious little to share, and sometimes lack even the basic necessities of life.

Communist theory, of course, declares that everyone will have everything he needs when comrades share equally. Workers in Communist countries, according to theory, share ownership of both their factories and the product of their labor. The Communist Party is supposedly just the service organization which makes sure no one claims anything as his own private property.

Communists, for their part, disdain the rest of the

world as too selfish and too "reactionary" to appreciate their envisioned Utopia. Thus they must conquer the world in order to impose the Utopia everyone really needs. Universal peace will finally come only through the establishment of an earthly paradise wherein all things are shared equally.

In reality, communism, once imposed, produces results quite different from those predicted by Communist theory. Instead of people controlling their own lives and their society, they end up controlled by a *totalitarian* state (not merely an authoritarian one). In that state a privileged few gain control of all power and all wealth. This, of course, is supposed to be a temporary situation, leading eventually to the promised Utopia. In his book, *How Should We Then Live?*, Frances Schaeffer comments: "Over a half-century has passed and not only have they not achieved the goal of 'communism' anywhere, they have not even come to a free socialism. The 'temporary dictatorship of the proletariat' has proven, wherever the Communists have had power, to be in reality a dictatorship by a small elite—and not temporary but permanent. Communists have had to function on the basis of internal repression."[2]

This repression works at many levels of life in Communist countries. Information is repressed. The teachings of communism are aggressively propagated to the exclusion of all other viewpoints. Opposite ways of thinking are not merely prohibited but severely punished. According to the "Party Organization and Atheist Education," a magazine article published in 1975, 10 million people out of the population of 260 million in Russia have been trained to spread atheistic propaganda. This includes 1.2 million propagandists, 2.05 million trained public speakers, 1.8 million informants and 3.7 million agitators.[3]

Little wonder, then, that the church in Eastern Europe is constantly oppressed by stringent censorship and propagandist attempts to undermine its faith. And it is precisely in that grim context that the Eastern European Bible Mission ministers to Eastern European churches.

The Communist Takeover

Just how did this nightmare begin? Communism as we know it today first took root in Russia. But it was not the Communists who initiated revolution there. Rather, it began with the February Revolution in 1917, led by Prince Lvov. Lvov was succeeded by Alexander Kerensky. Kerensky, like Lvov, was a social reformer, not a Communist.

Immediately after the February Revolution, Stalin hurried back to Russia from Siberia, Lenin from Switzerland, and Trotsky from New York. Then in October, 1917, the "Bolsheviks," as these three Communists and their followers were called, wrested control and initiated a rule of repression. The next month, these Communists, thinking they had popular support, permitted the first free election ever held in Russia. To their utter horror, they won only a fourth of the seats. Yet when the resulting assembly met for the first time in January, 1918, Communist troops scattered it by force.

No free election has ever been held in Russia since.

By this time, representatives of factory workers in Petrograd were already cursing the Communists who, they said, had deceived them. The Communists had earlier abandoned Petrograd to cold and hunger and fled to Moscow. The troops they left in Petrograd were ordered to "machine gun the crowds of workers in the courtyards of the factories, who were demanding independent factory committees."[4]

Before coming to power, Lenin had studied an earlier futile experiment in communism—the Paris Commune. Lenin pinpointed what he called the main reason for the Paris Commune's 1871 defeat. He decided it simply had not killed enough of its enemies![5] When Lenin himself, therefore, came to power, he immediately set up the machinery of repression. He saw correctly that there was no other way to set up a Communist regime in Russia. The Russian people had to be clubbed into accepting Communist rule. And a regime established with such malevolence could not easily become a benign regime later on.

How Communism Controls Society

Communism controls its subject societies by various means of repression and coercion. Lenin machine-gunned his opponents. Stalin terrorized millions with his purges. The Berlin Wall was built in 1961 to contain the East German population against its will. To keep their Eastern European neighbors under their jack-booted heel, Russian Communists used tanks in East Germany in 1953, in Hungary in 1956, and in Czechoslovakia in 1968. To prepare for their takeover of Poland, Communists secretly executed thousands of Polish officers and buried them in Katya Forest following the second world war.

In the Soviet Union, the control of society begins with the family. Parents are required by law to bring up their children in the "spirit of communism." The spirit of communism includes complete devotion to the Communist Party and asks that the concerns of the revolution and the Party be placed ahead of individual interests. A life lived in the spirit of communism is a life lived to propagate communism.

Communist indoctrination begins with three-year-old children. In preschool they are taught the value of collective rather than individual goals. In youth organizations as well as in school they are taught social discipline, respect for manual labor and love of country. In an article in the *International Herald Tribune,* Dan Fisher of the *Los Angeles Times* said that "virtually every Soviet citizen is a member of at least one of these" youth organizations at some point in his life.[6]

Young people are also subjected to intense media

pressure to conform to Communist ideology. This pressure often takes the form of anti-religious propaganda as it did one day in the daily paper of the Young Communist League. The paper devoted a full page to two long articles against religion under the heading, "Intellect Versus Religion."[7]

The first article was a reply to a letter supposedly sent to the paper by students at a technical college. Their roommate, Nadya, began attending Baptist prayer meetings and admitted openly to believing in God. The two letter writers were concerned about Nadya and did everything they could to bring her to her senses. But to no avail.

In the article, the reporter recounted his meeting with the two girls who wrote the letter and his talks with Nadya's teachers. He did not report a happy ending, however. Nadya was not "saved" at the last moment from the clutches of her Baptist friends.

Rather, she was described as a complex character who had a lonely childhood and found it difficult to make friends at college. This, claimed the author, made Nadya particularly vulnerable to the overtures of the Baptists.

The second article on the same page was prompted by the concern of a reader who lived near a Baptist church. He became very upset to see teenagers flocking to prayer meetings. He tried to argue with them, but found them "deeply convinced that they shall have life eternal in Heaven (moreover, that only Baptists will go to Heaven). What fanaticism!"[8]

The young writer asked that the newspaper publish some background on the Baptists. In reply, the newspaper first gave background on the official Baptist church in the Soviet Union. Then it mounted a heavy attack against the underground Baptists and other "sects present in our country."[9] The usual sinister picture of reactionaries who pervert the minds of children and youth was painted. These people, said the article, are unwilling to do their share for society at large, and violate Soviet regulations by their religious practices.

Job placement is still another means whereby the State exerts extreme pressure upon individuals. Only those whom the Party approves can hold supervisory positions, and usually Party membership is a prerequisite for approval. Even so, only six percent of the total Soviet population belongs to the Communist Party. A large percentage of the membership, however, is thought to consist of men between the ages of 30 and 60 who joined the Party in innocence before its ravages against human freedom in Russia became apparent—or for personal gain.

Christians are especially subject to employment discrimination. They are specifically prohibited from educational and supervisory positions. I personally know four people in a single Bible study group in Czechoslovakia, for example, who were demoted for their faith. Two of them had been professors, one a teacher, and the other a supervisor.

Even the queues (lines) in which one must wait for the basics of life are a means of controlling society. Menachem Begin, who was once a prisoner in a Soviet labor camp, says in his book *White Nights*: "The man in the queue is completely occupied with getting to the top of it . . . not returning home empty handed. His entire thoughts are concentrated on getting what is required for mere subsistence."[10] In this way even the queues may serve to occupy the leisure time which some people might otherwise use to plot against the ruling clique.

Preparing the Ground for Revolution

The avowed purpose of communism is to impose its definition of Utopia upon the whole world. This is called "setting the masses free." But before they can do this, they must rouse people from stupor. This they accomplish by infiltrating government, labor unions, educational institutions, social and health-care organizations, and even Christian organizations. Once on the inside, Communists begin spreading the false notion that communism champions scientific progress. At the same time they try to trigger economic depression and then pit class against class in the resulting chaos. Communists teach young people to blame society or their parents instead of themselves for the restrictions they experience. Freed of responsibility for the consequences of their own behavior, people begin to condemn the social structures around them. So strong is the Communist penchant for placing blame outside oneself that they accused Viktor Trstencky of "creating unrest" in 1974 when he preached about the eternal accountability of all men, believers and unbelievers alike, before God.

Communists focus special attention on minority groups in Europe, the Third World and North America. First they spread paranoia among the members of the minority culture. Then they malign the majority culture as oppressive. Result: minorities find themselves in a vacuum where Communist ideals seem to be their only option.

Results of Communist Propaganda

What is the result of all this effort to control people's thinking and foment revolution throughout the world? For the most part, Communist propaganda seems to find better acceptance among naive westerners than it does among citizens of Communist countries. A favorite joke even in Moscow itself involves a play on two Russian words, *pravda*, "truth," and *izvestia*, "news"— words also used as names for Russia's two leading state-controlled newspapers. Whenever an innocent tourist asks, "Aren't *Pravda* and *Izvestia* really the same newspaper?" Russians reply with a wink, "No. Izvestia is not Pravda and Pravda is not Izvestia—a covert way of saying what everyone knows: in Russia, "The news is not truth and the truth is not news!"

Communism's greatest problem in our day is not its external struggle against the West but rather the spreading apostasy within its own ranks. For example, a middle-aged Russian scientist is quoted by Dan Fisher as saying that "young people are cynical opportunists. They no longer believe in Marxism-Leninism, but say they do to advance their careers." The young are restless. For them the only heroes communism offers are tired, stone-faced old politburo members who are no longer capable of providing adequate inspiration.

In Poland early in 1981, though they had been reared since infancy on Communist propaganda, tens of thousands of Polish university students staged sit-in demonstrations protesting the fact that both Marxism and the study of Russian language are required subjects in Polish universities. They insisted that Marxism and the Russian language be offered as elective courses only. In the view of many this kind of intellectual protest is even more dangerous to communism than Solidarity's workers' strikes. And whereas Marx promised that the communizing of society would abolish economic depression, alcoholism, juvenile delinquency, absenteeism, divorce and high suicide rates, all these ills are afflicting Communist nations today about as much if not more than they afflict our own Western societies.

Eastern European economics are crumbling, rather than thriving, under socialist directives. The Soviet Union is no longer able to supply the energy needs of its allies. Just as in the West, consumer prices are rising steadily, causing workers to feel betrayed as they watch the purchasing power of their earnings dwindle. What, after all, has communism offered them? Their unrest, their grave doubts about the practicality (not to mention the humanness) of Marxist philosophy, have opened the way for spreading strikes by workers and students alike, as in Poland in 1980 and 1981.

Exasperatingly tight Communist controls over every

aspect of life can cause bottled-up emotions to explode into violence. For example, one day a woman got on a bus near a hospital in Romania. She had her two children with her. One of them had his head bandaged, having obviously just been treated at the hospital.

The woman had only enough fare for herself and one child. The conductor demanded the third fare, but the woman could not pay it. Neither could she leave one child alone on the street. So the driver ordered her off the bus. Suddenly the other passengers became enraged at the driver. A mob which even the police could not control soon gathered around the bus.

More policemen were called. Firemen finally dispersed the crowd with water hoses. But not before one policeman was injured and the conductor was so badly beaten up that he died en route to the hospital.

According to the reports we hear when we travel in Eastern Europe, people constantly try to escape from Communist countries. We are told that many try daily to cross the border from Romania to Yugoslavia. Rumor has it that as many as 10 people die each day and that 150 more are captured. We have heard that crowds of up to 250 people have tried to escape by rushing the border barriers, only to be gunned down en masse.

Though these figures may be inflated, they indicate what is on the minds of Romanians. These are the numbers which they themselves accept as valid.

Does communism really work? Do lead balloons float?

VII
Churches Under Fire

Busy as Communists are trying to keep their sinking ship afloat, they still find plenty of time to maintain pressure against the church. In fact, communism's anti-religious fist will be the last part of the corpse to stop twitching when communism finally lies on its deathbed. Communist propaganda, of course, denies that the church in Eastern Europe is a church under fire. And once again naive westerners, wide-eyed with childish credulity, swallow as truth statements which citizens of Communist countries spit out as propaganda. Westerners visit Communist countries and come home saying things look better, that communism has at last decided to work hand-in-hand with religion.

From the outside things *do* look better for the church in Eastern Europe. State-church relations appear to be the best ever in *some* countries. But this is only a surface appearance. Actually, an all-out war is still being waged against the church. The ultimate goal is the church's destruction.

From its inception, communism has viewed faith in God as its enemy. As quoted in the *Collected Works of Lenin*, Lenin wrote: "Our party program is in its totality built on a scientific, hence materialistic, world view. With the proclamation of our Program it is essential to say that it also contains the unveiling/revealing of the historical and scientific bases about the origin of the religious mystery. Pressured by the need, our program therefore contains the Propaganda of Atheism."[11]

Briefly, by this Lenin meant that God is only an imaginary mystery that man has contrived to meet his own need. Therefore, to make those under Communism believe in a "materialistic" world (i.e., that physical matter is the only reality), atheistic propaganda was necessary. Lenin attempted to support this ideology with historical and scientific reasoning.

A 1977 magazine article published by the Communist party in Hungary, a more liberal country, states that "the ideology of our party is just the opposite of the religious ideology."[12] This statement, obviously not printed for Western consumption, appeared in December of the same year Billy Graham visited Hungary.

Eradication Takes Time

The eradication of the church is the ultimate goal of communism, but Communist governments know they cannot destroy Christian faith instantly. Nor can the same anti-Christian restrictions be imposed uniformly in all Communist countries, for national conditions vary. Poland is a case in point.

In Poland 95 percent of the population is Catholic. Hence the vast majority of Poles give their loyalty to the church and merely tolerate the reign of communism as an unavoidable, though hopefully temporary, evil. They did not, after all, *choose* communism. Rather, Communists imposed themselves by force upon Poland when the country was too weakened by Nazi oppression to resist. In fact, Hitler's greatest evil was one he never intended—he gave communism its opportunity for expansion by weakening Eastern Europe. Communism

gained control there only through the default of nazi-
ism, not by any personal appeal it held for the masses.

Because of the sheer numbers of people who support
it, the Polish Catholic church is not afraid to voice its
opinion whenever the Polish Communists become
heavy-handed. As a result the Polish Communist Party
has become, however reluctantly, one of the most liberal Communist parties in the entire Soviet Bloc.

Another problem Communists face is that Christian
churches, if too severely restricted or outlawed, are per-
fectly capable of going underground! Large congregations simply break up into thousands of "spore congregations" and vanish into the crevices of society.
Without a visible structure the church becomes virtually impossible to infiltrate and control. Communists,
therefore, have learned to be more subtle—they give the
church just enough freedom to keep the "spore church"
phenomenon from happening, but not enough (they
hope) to allow it to flourish.

There are cases, even so, where the church *has* been
driven underground by too many restrictions. Probably
the best known example is the unregistered Baptist
churches in the Soviet Union itself. These churches, in-
cidentally, draw far more Russian youth into their
meetings than do their registered counterparts!

In 1960, under government pressure, the central
leadership of the registered All Union Council of Evangelical Christians and Baptists sent out instructions to
curtail certain church activities. Young people under
18 years of age were to be excluded from services! Baptisms of people from 18 to 30 years old were to be reduced to a minimum. And evangelistic preaching was
to be discouraged.

Feeling the leadership had gone too far in giving this
ruling, many Baptists reacted. They saw the directives
as inexcusable compromise—an attempt by their own
leaders to follow Christ and gratify the Communist

State at the same time.

Many Christians left the denomination and organized, in 1965, an unregistered Baptist movement. The leader they chose was Kryuchkov, a man who has since been in hiding for more than 10 years, living separate from his family as he secretly leads this fast-growing movement. When Georgi Vins became the secretary of the new organization, electronic "bugs" were planted in his home. Later the "buggers" arrested him and kept him in prison for five years (1974 to 1979). Finally he was stripped (without his consent) of his Russian citizenship and sent, along with four other prisoners, to the United States in exchange for two Soviet spies.

Still a third complication which prevents Communists from trying to eradicate the church in one fell swoop is world opinion in the West. To advance their cause around the world, Communists must try to maintain a good image. In other words, they must pretend that Lenin's and Stalin's disciples have managed to become greater than their masters by restraining their impulses to mass slaughter. Most Eastern European governments have signed the Helsinki agreement on Human Rights, and as members of the United Nations these Communist governments have strong influence within international peace organizations, including those within church bodies such as the World Council of Churches. To preserve an acceptable image in the West they must abide at least superficially by the Helsinki Accords. Their delegates will strongly oppose any doubts or questions raised in such international organizations.

Solzhenitsyn once said, "[Communists] tolerate the church only to the extent that is necessary for political decoration."[13] A Soviet Christian told me, "We say that on the main street is where the flowers grow." Where official delegations and tourists visit, things look their best!

Communist Tactics for Destroying the Church

In the western world many people study how to help churches grow. But in the Communist world intensive study is devoted to an opposite quest—how to make churches dwindle and vanish. Let's look at some of the restrictions Eastern European Christians face to help us understand how communism is working toward this goal.

Initially in Russia it looked as if the promises of freedom for the church were true. Never had Russian evangelical Christians experienced so much freedom as during the first years of Lenin's regime. But all the while Communists were developing tactics for controlling and eventually exterminating the church.

Their first tactic was simply *to investigate the church.* Undercover agents began noting church leaders' activities, their friends, their contacts inside and outside the country, their personal weaknesses, their policy statements, their plans for the future, and even, whenever possible, their very thoughts. They kept detailed files on all pertinent data. Peace and freedom, meanwhile, reigned outwardly. But behind the scenes Communists were preparing for *war.*

Following the initial investigatory phase *they isolated individual churches from each other and from the outside world.* Communists know that Christians draw strength from their sense of community with millions of other Christians around the world. Hence any information from churches in the outside world is censored. One effect the ministry of Eastern European Bible Missions has had is to counteract this part of Communist strategy. But Communists apply the principle of isolation even further within each leftist country. They isolate one denomination from another, one church from other churches, and one church member from other members. They discourage fellowship between churches and believers at any level.

The only way to break through the isolation is to break "the law," as Communists call their expressive edicts. And that's exactly what one group of seminary students decided to do. Forbidden to have group meetings outside their official classes, they decided to meet every day in the park, sometimes as early as 5:00 in the morning for secret prayer meetings.

At the same time public propaganda seeks to isolate Christians from society in general. Books, newspapers, radio and television, schools and learned commentators all devote an amazing amount of time and energy to criticizing the church and its leaders. Religion has a very bad press in Communist countries.

Having forced Christians into comparative isolation from society, Communists then gleefully point to their isolation as proof that they have voluntarily withdrawn from the real world. They stereotype Christians as people who prefer to live in the past, who stay out of touch with progress, science and new developments.

Communists even seek to isolate Christians from their own spiritual leaders. In countries like Czechoslovakia, they forbid pastoral care through visitation and counseling. Those who seek midweek contact with their pastors risk repercussions. A pastor who holds unauthorized meetings may promptly find his government-issued pastor's license revoked.

Communists emphatically try to isolate pastors from the young people. In Russia and Bulgaria, church attendance, religious instruction or counseling for those under 18 is totally forbidden. Czechoslovakia allows pastors of major denominations to give religious instruction but only in the context of atheistic schools, and then only upon a written request from both parents of any given child. Parents who make such a request, however, are soon called in for an official reprimand and later experience job discrimination. The future of the education of children thus instructed becomes unsure and the children themselves are publicly ridiculed for their old-fashioned beliefs.

Communist agents even discredit religious leaders before their own congregations by spreading false rumors about them. Pastors may be called in on short notice for interrogation regarding some trumped-up charge supposedly submitted by an unnamed parishioner.

On the other hand, Communists see to it that church leaders who have discredited themselves because of alcoholism, immorality or financial dishonesty are not removed from their pulpits. On the contrary, such pastors are the ones most likely to be promoted to higher positions in denominations or to larger churches in the main cities. At the same time Communists remove faithful pastors from big cities to small villages to minimize their influence.

The Communists do not permit pastors or seminary students to meet other pastors or students without special permission except on a one-to-one basis. Normally, pastors may not exchange pulpits even for one service, or officiate at a wedding ceremony in any church other than their own without special government permission.

As if their policy of isolating the church were not malicious enough, Communists also *intimidate Christians personally*. Pastors are intimidated by Communist demands that they fill in endless reports. This is true even in the more liberal Communist countries. Every activity must be reported. Baptisms must be reported along with the names of every baptismal candidate.

Nor may a pastor trust the superintendent or bishop who is over him in the government-controlled church hierarchy, for such men in many cases value their appointments by the State. Secret police even infiltrate the congregations. "Visitors" from the government sometimes tape services or take notes in shorthand.

I remember one occasion when an East German pastor managed to get around the official directive prohibiting summer Bible camps for the young. I was in his church with an EEBM team when some agents from the government arrived to check things out.

Communists had emphatically rejected Pastor Rudolf's request to hold a youth camp the previous year. So the next autumn when he submitted the government-required "plan for the church year" he included plans for a congregational "Church Emphasis Week." Government agents voiced no objection, so when the time came, news spread by word of mouth. During the specified week, young people, 400 strong, flocked to a nearby secret campground. They all attended the Church Emphasis Week as visitors who just happened to camp in the area.

Communist authorities, of course, quietly slipped into one of the evening meetings to see if everything was "in order." Watchful Christians, however, recognized the government agents and managed to pass a warning to Pastor Rudolf. Meanwhile a feeling of apprehension spread through the congregation.

"Two agents are in the balcony," someone whispered to me. "And two more are outside in a car."

Nothing unusual happened until the service began. Pastor Rudolf then stood up and gave his usual greeting to the congregation. He took pains to mention the presence of visitors from various cities in East Germany, Czechoslovakia and Hungary, the United States, Canada and Holland. Then he added, "A very special welcome to the representatives of the government who are with us tonight!"

I gasped, wondering what would happen next. Then I realized that this was Pastor Rudolf's way of warning the congregation to be careful. He went on to remind the authorities present that the world was watching and it was in the State's interest to let the service go on unhindered.

"We are grateful," he said, "that we can meet together in freedom, and that the whole world, through the eyes of our foreign visitors, can witness our freedom!"

The government agents soon left without incident that evening.

Often, however, the State's intimidation is more successful than it was in Pastor Rudolf's case. Though a single incident of intimidation may have little effect, repeated instances instill fear, much like repeated small pricks of a needle can cause sensitivity to the very sight of a needle. No need to use a gun on the church when persistent "needling" hopefully may do the job!

At irregular intervals, the secret police make unexpected "friendly visits" to pastors to check into their activities and plans for the church. These investigations sometimes take a whole day of the pastor's time. Then come visits from church leaders higher up the echelon, seeking to correct the local pastor who demonstrates "too much evangelistic zeal" or an "unhealthy interest" in winning the young to Christ. It is the task of these leaders to be sure State-church relationships are not jeopardized.

Besides pastors, Christian parents are subjected to intense intimidation. Even though adults may attend church, in Russia it is illegal for parents to take their children to church or to give them religious instruction even in their own homes. Communists warn parents who disobey this law that their children may be taken from them and sent to government boarding schools. Though the children are not often actually taken, the mere threat is a grave form of torture. One widely publicized case can frighten Christian parents in an entire city. Yet even the authorities must be careful not to overdo it or the registered churches may go underground, beyond government control.

Communists also impose puppet hierarchical structures. Not content merely to intrude into the privacy of parent-child relationships they even tell the churches what form or organization they must adopt. A church structure similar to that of the Catholic or Orthodox church hierarchies is imposed arbitrarily upon all denominations, even Baptists, Brethren and Pentecostals who usually prefer local leadership by elders. In the Soviet Union, Bulgaria, Romania, Hungary and Czechoslovakia the State retains the right to approve or not approve each church official in the imposed hierarchical structure. Naturally the creation of an echelon dangles before its members the temptation to vie with one another for higher positions. And Communists deliberately encourage such competition as a means of killing the spiritual vitality of Christian leaders. In most countries all members of the hierarchy become government-salaried employees who must, to retain their salaries, represent the new socialist way of life. These leaders, then, are especially subject to the next Communist tactic for weakening and destroying the church.

They tempt Christians to compromise biblical standards. Communist governments encourage compromise in a multitude of ways. Under the pressure some Christian leaders do compromise, for example, by abandoning their attempt to influence the young for Christ—the activity which most irritates the church hierarchy and the State.

Strong Christian leaders who refuse to compromise are usually not martyred, or even imprisoned, since this would have the effect of arousing other Christians to an impassioned rejection of government control. Sometimes they are simply encouraged to emigrate to the West. By such an act the government forestalls dissent, robs the church of a strong leader and, at the same time, polishes its image in the West by its apparent liberality in allowing a dissenter to leave.

However, the main purpose of a Communist State is not to rid the church of leaders but to press its leaders into conformity with the Communist mold. In this way the church can be weakened from within until it is no longer truly a church.

Sometimes better pay is promised as a reward for compromise. "Hank, the police visited me this week," said Daniel, a Czech pastor, one day. "They said if I stop working with youth I will get a salary raise." Daniel shook his head. "I always thought you should get a raise for working *harder*! Here, the *less* you work, the more you get paid!"

In Czechoslovakia another temptation to compromise has come through the organization of *Pacem en Terris* (peace on earth), a "peace organization" within the Czechoslovakian Catholic Church. Communist secret police founded *Pacem en Terris* in the first place, and some are still listed on its membership roles even today. Communists labored long and diligently on the constitution of *Pacem en Terris.* During meetings, state secretaries take detailed minutes. State representatives select the speakers and set guidelines for speeches. They decide who should lead discussions and what they should discuss. They dictate the final communiqués issued at the end of the conferences. Theoretically they could save themselves a great deal of time by simply issuing the communiqués without bothering to hold the conferences.

Obviously, *Pacem en Terris* does not have the interest of the church at heart but serves the politics of the State. This group's primary task is to encourage pro-Soviet peace movements in the West.

For church leaders, pressure to compromise begins at the seminary level. To begin with, only a very limited number of men are permitted to apply for seminary entrance. And each applicant must be individually approved by the State.

Secondly, the number of seminaries is severely restricted. Only three seminaries exist in the whole of Czechoslovakia! One serves almost all Protestant denominations, and two are Catholic seminaries. In addition, the Czech Hussite Church and the Slovac Lutherans have very limited training facilities.

In the Protestant seminary, the course lasts five years. Enrollment is limited to only 60 students, yet 12 professors form the faculty. The students take all classes together with the exception of a few hours which focus on denominational distinctives.

Seminary students are encouraged to report on one another, as well as on their professors. Both faculty and students are required to pledge full cooperation with the government. The professors are paid by the State, with the intent that their first loyalty shall be to the State.

Concerning this dismal setting, Jiri, a seminary student, commented: "We think two or three of our professors may be born-again Christians, but most are stooges of the State and contribute to still further Communist infiltration of the church." The situtation Jiri reported is said to be even worse in the Catholic seminaries. As a result, in October, 1980, 120 out of 140 students in a Catholic seminary in Bratislava went on a two-day hunger strike to protest secret police insistence that they join *Pacem en Terris.*

Finally, Communists seek to discourage Christians by *ensnarling the church with nuisance regulations.* To begin with, local pastors must be licensed by the government to preach. And their license may be revoked at any time. In the 10 years following the 1968 Russian invasion of Czechoslovakia, Communists revoked the licenses of more than 500 pastors and priests and then fined or imprisoned them. They were charged in most cases—for holding illegal Christian meetings!

According to regulations, official aid from Western

churches, whenever it happens to be sent, must go only to registered churches. Much of it goes directly to the loyal central leadership. The underground church and unregistered lay movements get nothing. They are also the ones who have the greatest difficulty securing Bibles. In these new lay movements, Bible study is the central part of their meetings. They need millions of Bibles to meet the growing hunger for the Word of God.

Communists rigorously censor religious materials. It is a rule of thumb that the more stringent the censorship in a country, the fewer Bibles there are. Those who are found with a Bible which was printed in the West may be fined. If quantities of Bibles are involved, imprisonment may result. In Romania, for example, 20 people were arrested for possessing Bibles printed in the West. Five of the 20 received sentences ranging from one-and-a-half to five years for distributing such Bibles.

Neither is the church permitted to operate its own printing equipment. In most of Eastern Europe there is no legal way to produce any Christian literature. Even church typewriters must be registered with the authorities in some countries to have full control over *any* means of duplication.

In less restrictive nations, literature may sometimes be printed by a denomination, such as in the Hungarian Reformed Church. It is sent to local churches, whose members are *required* to buy it. "But no one reads it," says Peter, a pastor in the Hungarian Reformed Church. "These things aren't worth reading by the time the censors get through. They just produce money for the central church office and make good propaganda for the West."

Evangelism in Eastern Europe is confined, by law, to the church building and may occur only during regular worship hours. Sharing one's faith on the street or even in one's own home can mean immediate imprisonment in the more restrictive Communist countries. Imagine how small churches in the West would be if Christians witnessed only within the walls of the church at scheduled worship hours!

Lay involvement in churches is also forbidden. With rare exceptions, Christian ministry must be limited to priests or pastors, may occur only on Sunday, and may be directed only to the old and poor.

As if the church were some x-rated institution, work with youth and children is strictly regulated or even forbidden. Rallies and camps so familiar in the West can only be held secretly in many Eastern European countries.

Pastor Peter, mentioned above, told me his bishop would not allow him to hold separate youth meetings. "Jesus' body is one, so the youth cannot be separated from the rest," the bishop argued facetiously.

The foregoing is a summation of Communist tactics as many Eastern European friends have reported them to me over the years and from much documented personal research. I also include an abbreviated report written by Professor A. Hlinka, a Czechoslovakia Catholic now living in the West. He enumerates the following steps as the means whereby Communists placed the church under their heels when Czechoslovakia was overwhelmed by communism in 1948.[14]

1. Initial freedom for everyone.
2. Nationalization of schools.
3. Curtailment of printing presses.
4. Arrest of influential church leaders.
5. Division of the church—Catholic from Protestant and Czech Catholic from Slovak Catholic. Effort made to include church leaders in the new government.
6. Confiscation of many church-owned properties.
7. Replacement of school teachers and college professors who were religious.
8. Absorption of Christian women's organizations

into the Communist women's organization.

9. Church isolation from the West. Leadership shuffled to include only those loyal to the State.

10. Christians removed from influential jobs; many imprisoned or sent to labor camps.

11. Police interference in church districts which were taken over by the State with promises of no interference!

12. All church documents and statements examined and subjected to State approval.

13. Permission required for meetings of church leaders and any other special meetings.

14. Remaining freedoms taken from churches. Opposition imprisoned. Church leaders made employees of State. Clergy paid minimum wage by State to engender dependency. Community Party members installed as the head of State Office of Church Affairs.

15. Lay people relegated to mere spectator roles in church.

16. Liturgy led only by State-approved people. Up to five years imprisonment instituted for priests who hold meetings without permission. State approval required for candidates to fill posts of bishop and seminary professor. All religious leaders required to give a promise of loyalty to the State.

17. State approval required for church budgets.

18. Control of remaining church property by State.

19. Organization of *Pacem en Terris*, leading to false representation of the church to the rest of the world.

20. Thousands imprisoned, sent to a labor camp or killed, leaving the church in large measure intimidated and fearful.

In 1968 after Russia invaded Czechoslovakia, Communists focused attention upon individual Christians and their families. Most young pastors were fired, leaving priestly and pastoral duties filled largely by older men. Individuals in all churches were encouraged to spy on one another, giving the State even more control over the church.

The Condition of the Church

What then is the state of the church in Eastern Europe? According to Josif Ton, a Romanian pastor, "Evangelical Christians are increasing rapidly despite all opposition." EEBM finds a great spiritual vitality not only among adult Christians but also among the young. In reality, communism is struggling against a peaceful Christian counterrevolution within its own borders, and none of its weapons against that revolution have proved successful. In every country controlled by communism people continue to turn to Christ even after more than 30 years of Communist oppression! (More than 65 years in Russia.)

Josif Ton believes that Christians have a special role to play within the socialist system. He states, "The fact that religion is not vanishing under socialism, but rather growing in strength, must cause, sooner or later, a revision . . . of the Communist Party's attitude toward this aspect of individual and social life.

"Che Guevara, the passionate revolutionary, said, 'If socialism does not mean the transformation of man's character, it does not interest me, . . . Socialists have tried many ways to achieve this end. Why does it not allow Christ the opportunity to prove His power to transform men? Jesus Christ is not an enemy of this society; He is its only hope! . . .

"We believers have a place in the socialist state. God chose us to follow Him from *within socialism*. . . .

"The divine task of the evangelical Christian living in a socialist country is to lead such a correct and beautiful life that he both demonstrates and convinces this society that he *is* the new man which socialism seeks."[15]

The church under communism, then, is alive and growing—despite its struggles. God has His new men and women who radiate His love in spite of intense persecution.

VIII
Christians Under Fire

"Do you know why Russia invaded Czechoslovakia in 1968?"

"They were invited."

"And why are they still there after all these years?"

"They're still looking for the person who invited them."

So goes just one of numerous "Russian jokes" which the captive people of Eastern Europe tell to mock their Russian oppressors (though not usually to their faces!). Communism controls Czechoslovakia only by the sheer weight of Russian armed forces still present in the country. And Poland would throw off her heavy Communist yoke in a day were it not for the presence of several Russian divisions within her borders (and the possibility of other divisions invading from just beyond her borders). And of course the fact that disobeying Communist regulations can lead to interrogation, imprisonment or even death casts its pall of depression on the normally joyful peoples of captive Eastern Europe.

Piotre

Piotre, a Russian pastor, is a shining example of the

many believers who have proved more than a match for the politburo's henchman. Some 20 years ago, Piotre began ministering God's Word to an unregistered group of about 20 people in a certain Soviet city. Soon their number increased dramatically, for the life of the risen Christ was winsomely manifested among them. Communist police soon got wind of the movement and called Piotre in for interrogation.

"This must stop!" they told him. "It is illegal to evangelize in Russia. People must be free to make their own choices."

But the church continued to grow. Police observers came around more frequently. Soon the police began harassing Piotre with as many as three interrogations per month.

"You have got to stop this," the police kept saying, "or you will end up in prison!"

"If that's what you think is right," Piotre said calmly, "put me in prison."

Time passed. Piotre never changed his ways, and his ministry flourished. The church kept right on growing.

"You are headed for labor camp in Siberia," the police threatened finally.

"If that's what you think is right," Piotre said quietly, "send me to Siberia."

One day, while interrogating Piotre, a Communist officer became livid with anger. He didn't know how to handle Piotre's calmness. His hand slid to the holster at his belt and he quickly whipped out his pistol.

"You'd better start doing what you should or I'll shoot you!" he shouted, pointing the gun at Piotre.

Piotre looked down the barrel of the pistol. It was just a few feet from his face. He knew this could be the end. "Before you shoot me," he asked quietly, "may I have five minutes to pray?"

The officer turned pale. His pistol arm dropped limply to his side. "Get out!" he raged.

Piotre stared at the man for an instant. Then he

turned and walked out. A short time later he found himself "sentenced" to be a street sweeper! Every day he carried a broom through the city streets, clearing grime and garbage from gutters—and radiating the joy of Christ all the while. Since personal harassment of the shepherd had proved ineffective, Communists began pressuring the lambs of his flock. Included among the pressures was something the Communists hoped would serve as an enticement—an offer of official recognition for the church if only it would stop evangelizing and baptizing people.

"We'd rather stay unregistered," Piotre answered simply.

Over the course of the years the police personally threatened many members of Piotre's group. Some were even imprisoned. A few went all the way to Siberia because of their faith. But the church never faltered; and it continued to grow. Finally, weary of trying to intimidate the group, the government granted it official recognition without demanding any compromise!

"Persecution is good for the church," Piotre told me when he had finished telling his story. He was as casual as a doctor prescribing a regime of exercise for a patient. "Actually, it's good to have seasons of freedom for a wider proclamation of the gospel. But it helps if seasons of freedom are followed by times of persecution to weed out halfhearted people who really don't belong. I feel sorry for churches that never experience persecution. How do they manage?"

"While the government was pressuring you and your congregation," I commented, "you were busy evangelizing. How did you manage to do it?"

"We cannot hold city-wide evangelistic campaigns as you do in the West, but," Piotre grinned, his eyes sparkling, "we have our little ways. We teach our people that *everyone* among us is a witness. Our elderly women, for example, keep graveyards. They go individually to people who bring flowers and are grieving over the graves of loved ones and talk to them about death and eternal life. Many people are much more serious-minded and realistic at such times.

"But most of our members are younger," he continued. "They use other methods. We make every rite of passage in our lives a time to invite many guests and preach the word clearly. For example, it's common to have 500 to 800 guests at an all-day wedding of one of our members. They all hear the gospel before they leave! Bondorenko, a pastor with the Baptists, actually had 2,000 guests at his wedding! And they all heard the Word preached!

"Preaching at Christian funerals is another way we evangelize," Piotre added. "A graveside service may last an hour or two. Unbelievers as well as believers are there, and many believe as we preach. For every dear believer we lay to rest, we may gain 10 or more new believers to take his place!"

"What about your official church services?" I asked. "Are they limited to Sundays? I know how difficult it is for most churches to prosper on the few services officially allowed by the government."

"Oh, no," Piotre answered. "On Friday nights we have small-group prayer meetings all over the city. Monday nights we hold dozens of secret Bible studies. By appointing several laymen to minister in every official service, we have trained about 100 laymen who can preach and teach the Word. We also have youth meetings on Saturdays.

"Yes," Piotre smiled, "what we cannot do officially, we do secretly. In many cities the police even stand at church doors to turn the children and youth away as people are entering. Only in some of the big cities where Western tourists come is there more toleration—for show.

"About 600,000 Baptists and 40,000 Pentecostals attend registered churches here in Russia," Piotre went on. "But many more such groups remain unregistered.

They believe the comparative freedom we have now cannot last long. They don't want to give away information about members by registering with the government. That information could be used against millions if a major persecution should be launched later."

Piotre was silent for a moment. Then he went on quietly, but firmly. "I want to use the measure of freedom we have, but I'm ready to go underground at any moment it becomes necessary."

Frank

Frank, a Czech Christian I met on the same trip, is just as fearless as Piotre. He handles police interrogations with marvelous humor.

Frank is one of the most colorful characters I have ever met. Though we didn't know each other, he welcomed me with a crushing bear hug, planting his unshaven cheek firmly against mine. Sixty years old, he works at night to supplement his meager pension.

"I'm the night watchman on a hog farm," he grinned. "I don't make much money, but I have a rich Father!"

We sat down to talk. The only language we had in common was German, and Frank spoke it atrociously. Still, I managed to understand most of his narration.

"They call me constantly," he said, exhibiting not the slightest concern. "They yell at me and threaten me because I get Christian magazines and Bibles from abroad. When they get really upset," he chuckled, "I say, 'Why do you scream at me? Can I help it if people send me things? If this literature is so forbidden, why did customs officials let it pass through customs? And for that matter, why has the national mail service agreed to deliver these items to my address?'

"They suspect that I receive and distribute quantities of Bibles," Frank went on. "I don't deny any of it. But when the authorities question me, I feign indignation and reply, 'Bibles forbidden? Nonsense! The gov-

ernment prints Bibles. And didn't Brezhnev allow President Nixon, on a visit to Moscow, to donate 200 Bibles
to the registered Baptist Church?' "

Before I knew what was happening, this irrepress-
ible Christian persuaded me to carry 400 Bibles from
his well-hidden supply to a secret address known to be
under police surveillance! We stashed the Bibles in my
car and I got into the driver's seat.

"Now, keep sending as many Bibles as you can,"
Frank said. "So many people ask me for Bibles and I
want to be able to help them all."

John Stefan

John Stefan, a Polish citizen, reported recently upon
the sheer determination of Polish Catholics to resist
Communist restrictions against religious freedom. The
Communist government of Poland decided a few years
ago to build a "model Communist city"—a city that
would be to the Communist world what Brasília is to
Brazil. The designers hoped, of course, that people
moving into the city could be directed into new patterns
of life more consistent with the ideals of the revolution.
Those new patterns excluded, of course, church buildings and church attendance.

Nova Huta, Polish for the "the new city," sprang up
among the hills and fields of Poland—all according to
plan—at least until the Communists moved *people* into
the city to live and work there. "People" in Poland come
in only one mixture—95 percent Catholic and 0.6 percent Protestant, with Communists making up about
three percent. Once in the new city, whether the Communists liked it or not, these were the percentages of
the new residents. Inevitably tens of thousands of Catholics got together to request permission to build a new
church. The request was denied. They made a second
request, and a third. All were denied. After all, this was
to be a model Communist city; a church would spoil it!

Finally the Catholics decided to take matters into

their own hands. They found a large lot, and actually began to build a very large church even though they still had not received permission. As they were getting ready to lay the foundation, Communist police descended in force. Shouting for the workers to disband, the police rushed in among them, swinging their sticks. The people scattered.

But early the next morning they were back in full force. Soon the police appeared again. They beat some of the people and scattered the rest.

Morning after morning this curious cycle of building, beating and scattering continued until, sadly, five determined Catholics *died* from police beatings.

At that point the Communists gave in.

"We can't beat all of them to death," a government official finally said. "There are more of them than there are of us. Very well, let them build their church—but only *one*, mind you, only one!"

So they built only one, mind you, only one! But it held about 4,000 people (standing, not sitting in comfortable pews). Eager Catholics fill that church from vestibule to vestry with 16 consecutive services every Sunday! In other words, between 6:00 A.M. and 10:00 P.M. on a Sunday, 64,000 communicants spend an hour each inside that one church. The alternate Sunday 16 totally different audiences of 4,000 people each fill another 16 services! Thus 32 congregations of 4,000 people each use that one church building every fortnight. And still the whole congregation cannot get inside the church even on two consecutive Sundays.

With 141,000 members, that long-forbidden church in the "model Communist city" of Nova Huta was for a time the largest single congregation in all of Christendom. Only in the last few months of 1980 did a Protestant church in Seoul, South Korea, pass the Catholic church in Nova Huta in size; interestingly, the rapid spread of Christianity in South Korea is also, in large measure, a reaction against the threatening presence of a Communist government in North Korea! How Communists must grind their teeth to see how much they contribute to the growth of Christianity!

John Stefan reported also that Communist authorities recently leveled thousands of fines against thousands of Polish homeowners. Which homeowners? Those who "illegally" gave lodging to Protestant and Catholic youth participating in "illegal" summer Bible camps sponsored by "The Oasis Movement" (a renewal movement wthin the Polish Catholic Church). What was the response of both the homeowners and the youth? They mailed in the fines in postal money orders of about $1.00 value each. The office designated to receive them quickly filled to the ceiling with mail sacks. No further fines were levied.

Conflicting Reports: Who's Right?

Some reports brought from behind the Iron Curtain paint a rather different picture, stating that Communists have already come to terms with man's religious nature and changed their policies accordingly. People often ask, "Hank, what should we believe? Our own denominational leaders visited Moscow and came home saying there are no longer any major problems for the church in Eastern Europe."

Others ask, "Do you really need to smuggle Bibles into Eastern Europe when the Bible society is meeting the need through official channels?"

"What do you think about Billy Graham's visits to Hungary and Poland?"

"The leader of the Moscow Baptist Church and the president of the Romanian Pentecostal Church were in the U.S. Can't we trust their reports?"

The truth of the matter is that the only pastors and church leaders whom the Communists allow to travel to the West are those who have compromised by giving their first loyalty to the State. If they reported differently, they would forfeit their "special" privileges before the government (and perhaps also the security of their families in Eastern Europe).

Also, many Eastern European Christians have told me it is a "known fact" that some of those selected to represent their churches to the West actually work with or are *members* of the secret police. These individuals follow secret police instructions to the letter to blunt the concern of western Christians. Communist authorities know that when people hear conflicting reports they will not reach out with helping hands to their isolated brothers and sisters in the East.

And what of western denominational leaders who visit Russia and other Eastern European countries? To be sure, Communists love to invite respected western leaders to visit Europe and Russia. They show such visitors the window dressing of apparent religious freedom and send them home believing there is nothing to be concerned about. And again our Eastern European brethren are left without help and encouragement.

If only some of those leaders could accompany me on secret missions to mingle with rank-and-file believers outside those showcase churches they would get a different picture. I am sad to say, but secular publications such as *Time* and *Newsweek* often report the Eastern European situation much more reliably than Christian leaders. For example, a recent *Newsweek* article concerning Lithuania reported as follows:

"Every Sunday, St. Theresa's Church bustles with worshipers of all ages streaming in for the Masses that are conducted alternately in Lithuanian and Polish. Outside, one eye cocked for Soviet authorities, peasant women do a brisk business selling rosaries, imitation-gold crosses and holy cards. No sooner had I begun taking pictures than one alarmed middle-aged woman ordered me away, assuming that I was a KGB agent. After we cleared up the misunderstanding, the woman apologized, explaining that Soviet authorities have been trying hard to keep Lithuania's Catholics on a very tight rein. 'They are trying to prevent what is going on in Poland from happening here,' she told me.

"Like the Poles, Lithuanians are overwhelmingly Roman Catholic. . . . The government's anti-Catholic policy is a very sore point. The Soviets permit only ten churches to operate in Vilnius, a city of nearly 500,000, and the church at the university is now a 'museum of science.' Priests are not allowed to teach religion to the young. Only one seminary, at Kaunas, offers training for the priesthood, graduating about twelve young men each year, and the KGB must approve candidates. It is not unheard of for priests to be waylaid and beaten by thugs presumably working for the regime.

"Lithuania's Catholics have long since found ways to cope. Believers who occupy state or party positions often avoid trouble by attending Mass in towns where they will not be recognized. The church conducts a small underground seminary, and many women who work in occupations such as nursing also belong to secret orders of nuns. . . . Soviets have restricted contacts with Poland: once routine visas for family visits are now granted rarely and grudgingly. Lithuania's Polish minority complains that letters from Poland arrive weeks late, if at all. 'I don't know what is happening with my family,' said one elderly woman who had not received a single note since Polish strikes began a year ago. Newsstands now sell only those Polish newspapers that authorities consider 'safe.' At political sessions for Lithuanian workers, Soviet lecturers stress the dangers of 'counter-revolution' in Poland. Anyone with personal ties to Poland is suspect—and the KGB has stepped up its surveillance."[16]

Also when Billy Graham visited Hungary, Christian media reports in the West tended to exaggerate the attendance at his meetings. Average attendance for his meetings was several hundred, except for one meeting attended by 12,000. However, to complete the picture, it should be noted that Communists permitted advance publicity about the time and place for his meeting to be issued only one day in advance! No billboard, radio or newspaper advertising was allowed. More importantly, what Billy Graham was allowed to do, no Hungarian evangelist has ever been allowed to do! We must remember also that Hungary is one of the more liberal of the Soviet Bloc countries. So also is Poland, the other nation Graham was allowed to visit.

Every year several missions to Eastern Europe work closely with various Bible societies, requesting that they publish tens of thousands of Bibles. We purchase the Bibles and take them into countries where Bible societies are not able to produce and supply them sufficiently to meet the demand.

Missions such as ours seek to supply Bibles only to Christians who would not otherwise receive them. Often they are members of the many unregistered movements. Meanwhile, Bible societies may supply very limited numbers of Bibles, mainly in the more liberal countries and then only through the *registered* church headquarters. Unfortunately, Bible societies do not have any control over the distribution within each country. Thus the work of the Bible societies and the missions are actually complimentary.

We can be thankful for the work of Bible societies, yet must recognize that Eastern European governments allow limited Bible society activity in order to maintain greater control over the church. Obviously, Bibles taken into countries unofficially are outside government controls.

Communist governments, as a condition for cooperation with Bible societies, require them to declare publicly that they disassociate themselves from Bible smuggling. That doesn't mean they *oppose* the ministry of missions such as EEBM. However, it sometimes looks as if they do, for Communist authorities encourage public argument between different types of ministries. Once again, this serves to keep the western church confused and inactive.

There can be no *open* distribution of Bibles in most of the countries because that would be "religious propaganda." In fact, in some cases, people must fill in formal application forms to receive a Bible. They then receive one only if any are available. More often, none are available. In the process, *their names and addresses are registered and noted by the government!*

As we begin to get a clear picture of the true situation let us shake off our confusion and begin to minister to our isolated brothers and sisters in the East. The church in Eastern Europe asks for our help.

IX
The Andrew Principle

Rain drummed on the roof of the car. I drummed my fingers on the steering wheel. And stared through the windshield. All I could see was the reflection of a wet Romanian road. Other members of our summer team waited nearby in a second car. A third carload had not yet arrived. What had happened to delay that third car? And where were the Romanian youth who were to rendezvous with us here for a secret Bible camp.

I looked around at my companions—Luke, a Canadian pastor, Becky, an American college graduate and Ioan, our Romanian guide. Ione sat calmly beside me in the front seat, seemingly undisturbed by the long wait.

We were parked in a little cup of a valley. High above us black ramparts of the Transylvania mountains towered in grotesque shapes. On such a day it was easy to image why so many legends about sinister occult forces had originated in that very region! This was, after all, the second time we had planned a secret camp for Romanian young people in this region. I recalled the first time when, a year earlier, we had waited in vain in a city square for our contact. It seemed as if some brooding supernatural resident of the region was determined to resist the occurrence of such a thing as a Bible camp within his domain. I could feel my disappointment over that earlier aborted plan returning. Had we journeyed all this way just to stare at these bleak mountains and listen to this splattering rain?

"Oh, for a cup of hot tea!" I sighed. But our only propane burner was in the missing third car, along with most of our tents and other camping gear.

Rain sloshed still more vigorously against the car windows. If we had gotten stuck in the middle of an automatic car wash I doubt that the combined force of all its hoses could have unleashed more water upon us than this storm! I opened my window just an inch to see more clearly, but the wind whipped cold raindrops against my face. I quickly closed the window and pulled my cap down over my eyes.

Only Ioan seemed interested in conversation. Since none of us responded with much enthusiasm he talked only in bits and pieces at first. But finally he warmed up to a stirring narration about his family's struggle to survive under communism—with their faith intact!

"The secret police arrested my father in the late 1950s," he said, "and sentenced him to 20 years of forced labor simply because he was a pastor. As it turned out, though, they released him after only eight years."

"*Only* eight years!" we gasped. Suddenly we forgot all about our own troubles. We waited with bated breath for Ioan to continue.

"Shortly after they sentenced my father they arrested my mother and all of us children and sent us to a different labor camp in the Danube delta. Living conditions in the camp were horrible and the labor was hard, especially for mother who was pregnant and also suffered from a heart problem. Learning of our desperate situation a friend of our family voluntarily got herself sentenced to the same prison in order to lighten our burdens.

"During this time our Communist taskmasters showed us no mercy. Finally my baby brother was born in the labor camp. But soon he contracted polio. In the midst of all our suffering God intervened miraculously, and our whole family survived!

"The Communists intended those horrible conditions," Ioan said solemnly, "to destroy our faith. But God used them to bring us closer together as a family and to strengthen our faith!"

I pushed up my cap and looked steadily at Ioan. If God could use such horrible circumstances for the benefit of Ioan's family surely He could accomplish some good purpose, not only for our overdue Romanian friends, but also for our EEBM team. And He could accomplish His own good purpose with or without the camp we had planned!

The rain still fell. Clouds hung just as low as ever in the cup-shaped valley. But suddenly, inside the car, everything was brighter and warmer. God was with us!

Luke began to sing. One by one we joined in. Soon we were singing heartily. Finally we prayed together, affirming our confidence in God and calling down His blessing upon our Romanian friends and upon our three fellow workers in the missing car.

"Let's pitch the tents we have and get our luggage out of the car," I said after we prayed. Team members from both cars joined me and soon we had moved the luggage out of the cars and under protective canvas. By the time we got back into the cars we were shivering. But now at least we could stretch our legs. But oh, for a cup of hot tea!

Becky rolled down her window and put her hand out. "The rain is letting up!" she exclaimed.

"Let's take a look around," I said a little later. We wandered among the trees, surveying our situation. This high valley was a lovely secluded place—excellent for a secret camp.

"I see a hut on the hill above us," Luke said, pointing

ahead. We climbed through the trees to an old, weather-beaten building. I tried the door. It opened, but with a loud protest from its seldom-used hinges.

"It's dry in here!" Luke exclaimed, looking around the dusty interior.

We were all huddled inside the shack when the young people began to arrive. Every one of them was soaked to the skin. Their boots were caked with mud.

"You should see the road!" one of them exclaimed.

"A sea of mud!" added another. "But we couldn't let anything keep us away!"

"They walked up the mountain," Ioan explained to Luke and Becky. "Fifteen miles." Then he turned to the new arrivals. "How was the first part of your trip?"

"Fine," one of them answered. "No questions anywhere. But we had to wait half a day for the train."

"And we slept in a dirty old shack last night," added someone else. "We've been climbing into these mountains since dawn."

Our present shelter soon brightened with the warmth and enthusiasm the young people brought with them. Any one of them could lose his job or be fined or imprisoned if authorities learned he had come to this camp. But one would never guess that such a threat existed as they chattered happily among themselves. Finally they began to sing. We joined in whenever they sang a tune we knew.

Becky stood looking out the door as darkness began to fall. "There's the other car!" she exclaimed suddenly.

"We were delayed at the border," our three friends told us when we ran outside to greet them. "But here we are!"

"Praise the Lord!" someone exclaimed.

Everyone worked busily for the next half hour. We unloaded the rest of our camping gear and set up the tents. With our accommodations for the weekend finally in order, we returned to the shack. Sitting in a circle on the floor, we enjoyed a meal of hot tea and bread.

The next three days were filled with the young people's joy in their fellowship together—and our satisfaction in sharing that joy with them. Each morning we began the day with songs of praise. And each day someone taught the group a new song which each could take home and teach to others. After prayer, we ate our simple breakfast of hot tea and bread, and then someone led a devotional study from Jonah. When the dishes were washed we plunged again into Bible study. At noon we sang again, then had our lunch of hot tea and bread, followed by another devotional from Jonah.

During the early hours of the afternoon we took time to play volleyball or go hiking. Refreshed, we gathered once again for more Bible study, singing and sharing. The young people soaked up the Bible study and fellowship like thirsty sponges. It was the first time in 30 years that their denomination was helping with a summer Bible camp for young people.

After three days we felt God's leading to transfer to another location. When time came to break camp, it was hard to say good-bye. We prayed together one last time, then sang a hymn. The young people climbed into our three cars to be driven down the mountainside to the train station.

The cars had barely gone when Romanian police arrived from a different direction. "We're looking for some Romanian students," they said. "Where are they?"

"Not here," one of the young men who remained behind answered. "We're all Hungarians."

The police asked a few more questions, checked our identification papers, and then drove away. God had taken care of every detail. He had even scheduled the departure of the students to precede the arrival of the police by minutes!

EEBM's Work

The youth camp in Romania is a good example of

several facets of Eastern European Bible Mission's work. It was largely accomplished by summer missionary volunteers from the West. It ministers to youth, a group about which we have great concern. And it is typical in that the resulting blessings flow two ways: our volunteers from the West minister blessing, but they return to the West full of eye-opening information and challenged commitments to share with their home churches in western lands, information which tends to stimulate spiritual growth among Western Christians.

EEBM has a full-time team of about 12 people in Europe. But every summer our group swells as 40 to 50 short-term missionaries (we call them SMPers) join us for one, two or three months of summer ministry.

How does EEBM recruit these short-term missionaries? Usually through one of our EEBM "associates"— people who have traveled in Eastern Europe themselves and help us part-time by speaking in Western churches on behalf of our ministry. Those who believe that God wants them to work with us and are approved by their local church must submit an application. Then those selected receive preliminary orientation in their home country. When they arrive at our European base their real training for the work ahead begins.

SMPers are all kinds of people: pastors, students, professionals, singles and family people. They leave their jobs or practices for a short time to be an extension of their local churches' ministries to fellow Christians behind the Iron Curtain.

Some SMPers spend their time in Eastern Europe ministering to pastors and lay leaders in small conferences and youth camps like the one in Romania. Others may have less contact with local Christians but take hundreds of Bibles and training materials and books with them on trips to Eastern Europe.

These summer programs have met more than just short-term needs. God has used them to lead many

SMPers into a long-term association with EEBM or with Eastern European Christians directly. Still others find their way into some other kind of long-term commitment to Christian service. All our full-time staff in Europe and the United States began as SMPers. Other summer missionaries, returning to their own countries, have continued to support our ministry financially, through prayer, or with their time and energy on a part-time basis. How we thank God for all of them!

The SMP program has low overhead costs because each SMPer pays for his own transatlantic flight and contributes toward his own living and travel expenses while with us. Crossing borders, they can say they are employed in their own countries. They are in Europe only as visitors.

A constant turnover of our border crossing personnel is necessary lest border guards begin to recognize certain people as regular visitors, arousing suspicion. Thus far EEBM teams have never been caught with literature except for the time Al Young and I were stopped at the Russian border. But even if they are, there is not the same danger that SMPers might have to give away crucial information about our ministry. Why? Because they simply don't know as much! Such information is deleted from their orientation so that if they are questioned they can reply in all honesty, "We don't know."

Best of all, every SMPer who sets out to minister to the needs of the persecuted church soon finds that church ministering to him! As a result, his own former commitments are updated. Personal faith begins to grow. SMPers return home with a new love for Christ, a widened perspective regarding His work around the world, a heightened appreciation for the Word of God, and a closer communion with the Holy Spirit.

"We bring you greetings from Christians in the United States and Canada," the SMPers say every summer in churches, home meetings and camps throughout Eastern Europe. And their words are translated into

Hungarian, Polish, Russian or some other European language. "We come from the church in the West to tell you that you have not been forgotten. Your brothers and sisters are praying for you."

Shortwave radio messages of encouragement from the West also reach Eastern Europe, and they are very helpful. But even greater encouragement comes through fellowship in person with Christians from non-Communist lands who care enough to visit their belabored brethren in the Communist world.

Communists constantly malign Christianity as a system that adds up to nothing more than "mere words." Expressing our concern in action is the best way to refute the charge.

EEBM, however, does not limit itself to the Summer Missionary Program. Our full-time team and one-year interns are involved year round with ministry in Eastern Europe. We take Bibles, books and Christian education materials for thousands of individuals and churches each year, while working on longer term programs as well.

We westerners must, however, be careful not to view ourselves as the great benefactors who deign to share their blessings with "poor" Eastern European Christians. For this is not the Spirit of Christ. Christ's way is not merely to share blessings but also to bear *burdens*. We do not go only to rejoice with those who rejoice, but also to weep with those who weep.

But before we can really care about the joys and sorrows of people who live under conditions so different from our own, we must sit with them and listen to their concerns. We must see things as they see them. We must experience something of the restrictions they face and learn their ways of overcoming those restrictions. From such an awareness of the people grows a tremendous love and respect for them. It is only from a position alongside them, as equals, that we can effectively share what we have to share.

The Andrew Principle

Andrew, the disciple of Jesus, offers a model for us in this kind of sharing ministry. Andrew has always been a challenge to me. Although he is mentioned only four times in John's Gospel, he has significantly influenced my ministry and the thrust of EEBM.

After meeting Jesus, Andrew could not keep the good news to himself. He had to share it with his brother Peter. By following Andrew, Peter found the Saviour and was himself eventually mightily used of God.

Once some Greeks who wanted to meet Jesus went to Philip, and Philip took them to Andrew. Together they went to Jesus.

Andrew is mentioned again at the feeding of the five thousand. When Jesus asked where food could be bought to feed the crowd, Philip said, "Why, Lord, 200 days' wages wouldn't buy bread for each person to have a little bite!" But Andrew's response was, "There is a little boy here who has five barley loaves and two small fish" (see John 6:1-9).

Andrew did not take the lunch away from the boy to impress his Master with what he himself had found. He didn't look for recognition, but was eager to serve without personal gain.

When EEBM teams minister in Eastern Europe, we want to serve as Andrew did. We avoid dominating Eastern Christians, emphasizing instead what *they* have to offer the Lord and one another. We give them Bibles and Bible-related literature to help them develop their own spiritual gifts and minister more effectively to those around them.

As a mission, we do not care to flood Eastern Europe with Western music groups. Rather, we seek to help Eastern Christians develop musical ministries of their own, combined with follow-up, youth camps, Bible study groups and pastors' conferences. Sometimes we are heavily involved in an area initially, but our goal is to delegate responsibility to national leaders, eventually working ourselves out of work in one area to begin in another. Through this process, we gain the confidence of the church. As their confidence in us increases, our opportunities for service multiply.

When I see millions of Christians in Eastern Europe without Bibles or study materials, and Christian leaders with little encouragement or help for their task, what I have to offer seems so little. Perhaps you have had the same feeling of inadequacy as you have given yourself to a ministry. The need is so great, and one gift looks so small.

However, Jesus did not tell the boy with the five loaves and two fishes that he had too little. He accepted what the boy gave Him and multiplied it to make enough to feed five thousand people. How encouraging to know God does not look at things as we do. He accepts what we give. I want to give myself to serve my brothers and sisters in Eastern Europe.

X
The Besieged Ones

"The situation in seminary is getting constantly worse," Josef said to me almost as soon as I stepped inside his Prague apartment. "I was full of hope when I started seminary," he went on. "I planned to start prayer meetings among the students but I soon learned that was impossible!" Josef said that few, if any, of the professors in the seminary could even be considered true Christians.

Finally Josef shook his head. "I'm just glad I still follow Jesus *in spite of* my seminary training."

As we talked on I asked, "What do you see as the future of the official Czech church?"

"It has no future," Josef said flatly. "Our only hope is in the secret Bible studies we hold in our own homes. And they're springing up all over the country. Some are Protestant and others Catholic. A member of my own Bible study group has a special ministry to the Catholic Bible study movement."

"God seems to be working in a special way among Catholics," I said. "Why do you think that is?"

Josef was silent for a moment. Then he said sadly, "I think it's because many of us are still afraid. The Catholics, however, have shrugged aside their fear."

Christian Leaders

Josef represents the first of the three besieged groups which EEMB feels especially called to help— Christian leaders. The primary need is the training of young church leaders. For, in Josef's opinion, the official seminaries are training leaders to destroy churches rather than build them. It is simply part of the Communist plan for the annihilation of Christianity within the Communist domain.

In other Eastern European countries the situation may be better, though not much. In Romania, for example, not enough Bible school students are graduating to take the place of elderly pastors as they retire. Only one in eight Baptist churches has a full-time pastor, with 850 out of 1,000 churches being led by laymen who lack formal training. (The denomination numbers about 220,000 registered and 30,000 unregistered believers.)

"Furthermore," a Romanian Baptist minister told me, "the average church member, even in rural areas, is now better educated than his pastor. The government will not allow university graduates to go to Bible school. It's *either* Bible school *or* university. Add to that the poor quality of the training in the Bible school, and you have dissatisfaction among pastors and church members alike."

In Romania, as in other Communist countries, the clergy often compromise with the State which employs them. In such cases, laymen often take their places as the real shepherds of the flock.

Petru, a young Pentecostal lay leader, told me, "There is such an age gap between the many young church members and the pastors, most of whom are over 60. Besides that, many times the pastorate is only a job for the pastor rather than a ministry to the Lord. Often the pastor has his wife as church administrator, and they're both paid by the government! In such situations laymen, often young intellectuals, take the lead, and so become the spiritual leaders.

"The way things stand," Petru continued, "pastors usually don't want to know if anyone is leading a youth ministry. For if they did know they must report it to the government.

"Right now there are some unlicensed men pastoring churches and being paid by the congregation. It isn't supposed to be allowed, but it's tolerated. It works well."

In Romania, church leadership will obviously pass more and more into the hands of laymen. "But who will train them?" Petru asked, looking at me challengingly. "Can you help us?"

Another segment of the church in Romania is the Romanian Orthodox Church. The Lord's Army is a secret home group movement which has grown up within the Orthodox church. No one knows for sure what percentage of the 20 million members of the church are involved in the movement, but estimates range from 200,000 to 500,000 with a similar number of sympathizers. The Lord's Army has been severely persecuted by the government and criticized by "official" church leaders. It is also completely bereft of any official help or training materials for their lay leaders. Still, their numbers continue to grow as they focus on Bible study, sharing, prayer and evangelism and a personal relationship with Jesus.

In Russia, according to an Orthodox priest I know, there are three basic groups of people within the Orthodox church. First are the simple women whose faith is expressed mainly in ritual practices. Next are the intellectuals who dream of non-institutional religion and often have a vital faith. A third group is made up of the dissidents who demand that their church leaders lead a struggle for religious freedom for the church and human rights for individuals.

It is from the second of these three groups, the

young intellectuals, that strong church leaders are now rising. They are the future of the church. We believe God has called EEBM to provide special help for this group also.

Christian Families

A second category of people who are besieged under communism and are therefore of special concern to EEBM are members of Christian families. Under communism, family ideals are often despised rather than valued. In Russia, on the basis of Karl Marx's teachings, marriage was initially considered "private prostitution,"[17] an institution of corrupt capitalism. Later, Communists found it necessary to introduce a code of family laws to "make things work better"!

Today, marriage and family in the Soviet Union are under tremendous pressure. Almost half of all marriages end in divorce. The divorce rate is rising in other Eastern European countries as well. Divorce among Christians is still almost unheard of, but the pressures on Christian families are in some ways even greater than on non-Christians because their values differ so drastically from those of the atheistic society around them.

Dmitri Dudko, a Russian Orthodox priest, once said that "having undermined faith in God, atheism has undermined all bases of social life. . . . Build a domestic church," he urged. "It is the realization of your faith in the family."[18]

Dudko was right. There is no more fundamental unit of the church than the family. In many Eastern European countries, Christian families who invite their friends to join them form the most basic of cell groups from which Christ's Body is built.

Western families have many resources available to them, such as Christian books, seminars, and study groups on family and child rearing. Such helps are nonexistent in Eastern Europe. The family struggles alone without benefit of teaching or other support.

Christian Youth

A third "besieged" category under communism is Christian children and young people, the future church.

Communists have put Ivan, the pastor I met on my first visit to Russia, and his family through personal difficulties. Because he taught his children the precepts of the faith, they were actually taken from the home and put in state boarding schools. When I asked Ivan what particular thing he would like to emphasize to western Christians, he focused quickly on the children.

"Tell them our greatest problem in Soviet churches is with the children," he said, looking at me with piercing eyes. "We, the parents, have chosen to follow Jesus. We're ready to pay the price. But pray for our children. Every effort is made by the State to bring them up as atheists, to tear them away from the faith of their parents.

"Tell westerners to pray especially for the children who have been taken from their homes," he continued. "Often the parents don't even know where the children are."

Sometimes the Christians themselves make strong public protests against Communist harassment of the family. Perhaps the most impressive such protest was written to the Soviet government on May 20, 1977.[19] Mothers from 139 Soviet towns described the sufferings of children in past Russian history, then went on to detail the discrimination, terrorization and beatings their own children still suffer under communism, which is supposed to right the wrongs of the past. They expressed their constant fear that parental rights would be totally revoked and their children arbitrarily taken from them. It was a cry to the government for human compassion. The signatures of over 4,000 mothers filled 163 pages!

Perhaps Communist governments are incapable of heeding such desperate cries. But may they at least reach our hearts in the West and arouse our concern!

EEBM's Strategy

We in EEBM seek to minister to these three besieged groups of people—church leaders, families and the young—principally by four means.

First of all we go to them, breaking their isolation from the outside world with personal contact and encouragement. We listen to their stories. In turn we tell them of the awesome things God is doing around the world—in other Eastern European countries, in the West, and on distant mission fields. We are better informed than they are about what is happening beyond their own national borders and even inside Eastern Europe. We emphasize their unity with this larger, worldwide Body of Christ.

Second, we also encourage unity among believers in the East—especially among church leaders. For Communists try constantly to divide one group of Christians from another.

Another of our strategies, of course, is *to provide Bibles, Christian books and training materials.* As we travel in Eastern Europe we hear constant pleas for such things. Pastor Georghe, a Romanian Baptist, said, "Most of all we need materials to train leaders and pastors. Right now we have nothing." Nick, a Pentecostal layman, said, "More than anything else we need Bibles and songbooks." Frank, my night watchman pastor friend in Czechoslovakia, said, "Send us as many Bibles and books as you can."

Josef Ton, who was one of only five evangelical leaders in Romania who has a university education, pointed out in a special interview published a few years ago in the West that "smuggling" has been the main source of literature for the church in Romania.

Unlike most Christian leaders in Communist countries, Ton has been heard in the West. In this interview he said in part: "We need the help of the Christians in the West. In the last 10 or 15 years, our Christian work . . . has been tremendously strengthened by . . . different Christian organizations in the West, who have brought us Bibles . . . and literature. . . .

"We, the Baptists, the Pentecostals, and the Brethren, were dependent upon the Bibles smuggled in by various organizations or by Christians who were willing to take the risk. . . .

"It is the same today. In many areas of the country we witness a revival; large numbers of people are being converted . . . and all these need the Bible. . . . Praise the Lord, we were able to give them a Bible . . . smuggled in by love and daring of our brethren in the West."[20]

In EEBM, when we take Bibles, books and training materials into Communist countries, we sometimes distribute them individually; but as a rule we give quantities to leaders who have a better idea than we of the need within their own areas. These leaders take a much greater risk by distributing the Bibles than we have taken to smuggle them into the country. After all, they cannot return to safety in the free West as we can.

About the need for Christian books Josef Ton spoke of this need also in his interview. He said: "Until 1965, there was practically no Christian literature in the Romanian language. . . . We are not allowed to print any Christian literature in Romania. But since 1965 various organizations in the West have started to print books in Romanian, usually books translated by people in Romania—the manuscripts being taken out and printed in the West and then smuggled back in. This way, we have *The Normal Christian Life; Man's Origin, Man's Destiny*; recently, we received the first complete concordance in the Romanian language.

". . . It is possible because we have brothers in the West who took pains to build up organizations to collect the money to print and smuggle Christian literature into our country."[21]

In Prague one night I met a young engineer who translates materials for us to publish in the West and smuggle back into Czechoslovakia. As we talked, he picked up a copy of Larry Christensen's *The Christian Family* in Czech.

"Could you possibly print this book in the West for us?" he asked. "We want to use it in our study groups."

I held the book carefully in my hands. Each page had been typed, photographed and from those negatives, printed onto photograph paper. I realized that for him it would take many days to make a single copy of the book.

A final strategy of EEBM is *to provide the means to print literature and duplicate cassettes (on a limited scale) within a country.* We may provide a secret press, stenciling machine or high-speed cassette duplicator.

As we have already seen, often books are duplicated by any means possible within Eastern Europe. In many countries, individual Christians devote their live to typing books, page by page, making several carbon copies each time. The copies are passed around for Christians to read.

But the risk is great, as we realized from news from this young engineer that this is the most sensitive area of EEBM's involvement in Eastern Europe. He told us that Communist police had recently located a secret press. "Fifteen people were arrested, and now they're awaiting trial." For bringing these duplicating facilities it could bring more severe penalties than Bible smuggling or any of our other activities. And for Eastern European Christians themselves it could mean years of imprisonment.

Yet because they feel such a tremendous need, they are willing to take the risk. The least we can do is share their risk by providing the tools they need.

XI
A New Way of Life

"Hello, this is Mona," said the American-accented voice on the phone.

"Yes," I answered. "May I help you?"

"I've been accepted for EEBM's Summer Missionary Program," she said, "and I need further instructions."

"Fine," I said. "Let me connect you with someone here in the office."

Mona came to EEBM a few days later; but I had just left for the United States on a speaking tour. When I returned to Holland she was gone, but I learned that she had indicated an interest in working more permanently with us.

"The Lord has given me such a love for the work here," she told our staff at the end of her SMP assignment. "If you should need a secretary within a few months, I would love to serve."

We did indeed need a secretary, and Mona seemed more than sufficiently qualified. Before applying for the SMP she had worked as an English language secretary at a child evangelism center in Holland. While there she had coordinated an international conference with participants from all over Europe. So when we had an au-

tumn reunion of European SMP alumni and Mona was
there, I made a point of meeting her.

Nothing in my life had prepared me for what I began
to feel when I met Mona. She responded warmly to my
greeting, and love was suddenly very much on my mind.
With great effort I pushed aside my emotions to talk
business.

"I understand you're interested in joining us as a
secretary," I said.

"Yes," she answered, smiling up at me. "I really love
this place. I believe the Lord wants me to be involved in
this ministry."

"When would you be able to begin?"

"Well, I promised Corrie ten Boom I would spend two
months with her," Mona said, ticking off two fingers on
her left hand. "And I promised to help some friends who
are missionaries in Nairobi. That's two more months,"
she said, touching two more fingers. "By March I'll be
free."

"Good," I said. "I believe that will work out just right
for us here too."

I kept noticing Mona the whole weekend. I couldn't
seem to keep my mind off her. I had had other
girlfriends, but none of those friendships had blos-
somed into anything serious. Now here I was, thinking
seriously about a girl I hardly knew. It didn't make
sense.

"Lord, I want you to give me the life partner you
choose," I prayed again, as I had so often in the last few
years. I had always been able to leave it at that before.
But this time I kept thinking of Mona as the person I
wished the Lord might choose.

I saw Mona two more times before she came to
EEBM in March. One day I visited *Tante* Corrie (as we
Dutch call Corrie ten Boom), and Mona was there, smiling and efficient. My heart did a flip-flop and I quickly
turned my mind to other things.

"I am *not* in love," I said to myself. "There is no such

thing as love at first sight!"

Another day Mona visited EEBM before leaving for Nairobi. Again I pushed my feelings aside, making an effort to be very businesslike.

While Mona was in Africa I wrote to her a few times. But I made certain to keep the letters official, dictating them to my sister who was my secretary at the time. I tried to ignore my feelings. "There is no such thing as love at first sight! Or is there?" I kept telling myself.

Finally it was the day of Mona's return to Holland. She was to come directly to EEBM, and I decided that as director of the mission I should, of course, be the one to meet her at the airport. I must admit that I took the long way back to the mission that day!

During the following weeks we found ourselves going out together on various occasions, and my feeing of attraction toward Mona kept growing. Finally I had to admit that I was actually in love. And I decided it was time to let her know!

"Mona," I said, feeling very nervous, "we must talk."

"Yes?" she said, looking up at me.

I took a deep breath. The blood pounded in my ears and I wondered anxiously how she would respond to what I had to say. "I've been attracted to you ever since we met," I said. "And I've been enjoying our times together."

A little smile began to play at the corners of Mona's mouth. I wondered fleetingly if she found my statements amusing. But I plunged ahead. It had to be said.

"I love you," I said simply.

Mona's mouth curved into a real smile. Her eyes danced, and a happy laugh welled up from her throat. "I love you too," she said.

"You do?" I asked breathlessly.

"Yes," she nodded. "I've also been attracted to you since the first day. Whenever I saw you it would just well up inside me. But you were so formal," she went on. "I just gave it to the Lord. I hid it in my heart, like Mary hid her thoughts about Jesus. I didn't tell anyone. But I thought a lot about you."

"Really?" I asked. I could hardly believe it. Mona nodded. We laughed together and began to compare notes.

I hadn't believed in love at first sight. After all, I had little idea of what Mona was really like. I didn't know if she had the right qualities to be my wife—or I the qualities to be the right man for her. But the Lord knew! He had allowed our love for each other to be nurtured in quietness during the past few months.

From that day on Mona and I spent many hours together. We shared times of recreation together, and we prayed and studied together too. Three months later I asked her to be my wife.

After a two-year engagement Mona and I exchanged marriage vows before God. Five weeks later, the day after our first Christmas as man and wife, we left Holland on our first trip together to Eastern Europe.

It was a frigid night in Czechoslovakia when Mona and I approached a certain town seeking the home of a Christian couple. Gusts of wind buffeted our car with flurries of snow, causing us to swerve dangerously on ice-glazed roads.

We entered the town not knowing where to go, for we had been unable to find a map. "Lord, guide us to the right place," we prayed.

I could sense Mona's excitement mounting. She peered out the window trying to read streets signs on darkened street corners. We seemed to be alone. The town's residents had already barricaded themselves against the cold night.

"There!" Mona exclaimed. "Isn't that the street?"

It was indeed. We turned and drove along slowly until we found the right house. Then we drove on a few blocks, turned a corner and parked. Getting out of the car we walked back to the house.

Carefully I tried the gate. It was locked. I rang the

bell. An old man appeared.

"We are looking for a certain couple," I said cautiously in German, giving him the names we had been given.

"*Gläubigen*? Believers?" he asked in German, his face lighting up.

"Yes!"

The old man opened the gate and drew us quickly inside. He took us into the house and put away our coats and shoes, all the while calling out to the family that guests had come. We put on the slippers he pushed toward us. (This is a Czech custom to wear them indoors.)

Other family members began to descend curiously from upstairs rooms. First came the couple whose names we had been given. They were the old man's daughter and son-in-law. Then the old man's wife and two grandchildren appeared. In a few minutes we were all seated together and began to get acquainted. While we sat talking, other people began to arrive one by one.

"You are just in time for our secret Bible study," our host explained. "You will share from God's Word?" he asked, and I nodded in agreement.

"Someone is sitting in a car in front of the house," a man said, coming in the back door. "I detoured a few blocks before coming in after I saw him there."

The old man went upstairs to watch the car from a darkened window. Downstairs we began the meeting quietly. Time passed slowly. Ten minutes. Twenty. A half hour. People continued arriving at the back door at regular intervals. Everyone's mind was on that car out front. Was it the secret police? Did they know about the meeting? I wondered if the man in the car had followed Mona and me.

After 40 minutes our watchman came down the stairs. "He's gone now," he said. "Go ahead with the meeting. I'll stay upstairs to keep an eye out in case he comes back."

The old man went back upstairs and the meeting continued. Mona and I conveyed greetings, as usual at such meetings. Then I shared some thoughts from the Word of God. We had a rich time of fellowship together. Then people began leaving, one by one, through the back door.

"Most of this group is Protestant," the old man told us afterward. "Tomorrow there will be another gathering comprised mainly of Catholics. Stanislav, a young priest who is new in this area, will be speaking. You must meet him!"

Mona and I were unable to attend the meeting the next day but we did meet Stanislav. His remarkable qualities impressed me immediately.

Stanislav was in his late twenties. God had already blessed him wonderfully, especially in ministry to 18- to 30-year-olds in a previous parish. So many received Christ that those over Stanislav in the church hierarchy, ever loyal to the government, decided to relocate him in hopes of curtailing his influence.

"They told me this is my last chance," Stanislav grinned. "I must conform or lose my preaching license. But seriously, I am willing to die, like a grain of wheat in the earth, so that Christ might produce fruit from my life.

"Actually, there's plenty going on with young people here too, but I didn't know that at first. I thought I was the only born-again pastor in the area. Then I learned there were already about 20 Bible study groups!

"The young people, including many intellectuals, are searching for the truth in God's Word," Stanislav went on. "You can't hold them back. If anyone tries to discourage them, they start their own Bible study groups and manage by themselves. Sometimes pastors help them, but usually the pastors prefer not to even know about the groups. If they know, they are supposed to report. Then the government sticks its nose in to interfere."

"Are you working with any of the groups?" I asked. "Or have you stopped organizing them since so many already exist?"

"Oh, I never stop," Stanislav laughed. "I'm working with my colleagues to start more groups. We have still more groups started already. Some are for couples. Others are for older people. Many of the groups in this area are mixed, Catholic and Protestant. The Protestants are more intimidated than we Catholics right now. Since they are fewer and more fearful, the government finds them easy to control. Their pastors are kept under close surveillance."

Another day, Mona and I met Daniel. Daniel is a young family man, a leading Catholic intellectual. He translates teaching materials for EEBM to take out, print, and smuggle back in.

"We Catholics are facing some tough decisions in the Body of Christ in Czechoslovakia," Daniel told us. "Slowly but surely our traditional Catholicism is declining. It will end. There are not enough trained priests to perpetuate it. The first question we face is—what new form should we adopt? Should we do everything through small illegal study groups? Or meet as extended families in our homes?

"What we really have here in Czechoslovakia," he continued, "are Christian 'gangs.' Not criminal gangs, but groups of people who meet to build up one another in the Body of Christ. We have been pushed in this direction by Communist prejudice."

Daniel echoed what Stanislav had said about the youth. "They are disillusioned with traditional religion," he said, "as well as with the claims of communism. Many are turning to the Lord through informal study groups.

"Every year for three years now we have had a secret conference for study group leaders. Last year we had 45 from Slovakia alone. At such times we exchange books we have gotten separately from people such as you and Mona. And we plan new moves for the extension of God's kingdom."

Then, summing up his report, Daniel exclaimed, "This is the ideal time in which to live! We are forced to seek new ways and new forms. Instead of being religious consumers, we have to *produce*. We cannot lean upon the past. We cannot leap upon the institution. Jesus Christ is the only one upon whom we can lean as our Source of life and inspiration!"

Several months after our talk with Daniel we heard that he was arrested. After his release a few weeks later I had a secret meeting with him.

"It was six in the morning when the police came," Daniel told me. "They shouted, 'Police! Open up!' When I opened the door, 20 of them burst into the house. I learned later that houses were searched all over Slovakia that day. They went through our house for 15 hours! They inspected every nook and cranny and even took picture frames apart to be sure nothing was hidden. They combed the house from one end to the other, and then went back over it again. They confiscated all my correspondence, took all the addresses they could find and all my books and my cassette collection. I have since learned that they had us under surveillance nearly a year. And they had bugged my telephone."

"What about the study books one of our summer teams delivered to you last year?" I asked. "Did you still have them at your house?"

"Yes, we still had them," Daniel smiled. "Stacked in that small room. My wife and I were praying about those books all that day while the police searched the house. Do you know," he said, smiling more broadly, "they never even looked in that room! Each group of police must have thought the other had searched the room. So all the books were saved. It was a miracle!"

Daniel paused and looked at me very seriously. "I hope you won't take my arrest as an excuse to stop helping us," he said. "At least 2,000 Bible study groups have sprung up around the country by now, and more are being started daily. We need all the materials you can provide for our Bible studies. We need them now more than ever!"

From Czechoslovakia, Mona and I traveled on to Hungary. As we approached a remote village near the Russian border I could hardly wait for Mona to meet Peter and Maria, his wife. Peter had been removed to this village by the hierarchy of the Hungarian Reformed Church, but his influence and ministry had really not been limited.

"Peter was the one I met during my first trip to Russia with Frans," I explained to Mona. "He was just starting to hold secret youth camps then and he shared valuable insights with me for my ministry throughout Eastern Europe. During those days, it was hard to find advice on how to minister in Communist-controlled countries."

When we reached the village we packed our car and walked to the little Reformed Church. We maintained a brisk pace, yet the cold made our winter coats seem very thin. Snow squeaked under our boots. Nearing the church, we joined a throng of people headed in the same direction. Inside the little building Mona and I separated. She sat with the women on one side while I joined the men on the other.

The building was unheated and I could see my breath writing the notes on the air as we started to sing. A lady played an old organ, pumping vigorously. I snuggled deeper into my coat as the service progressed.

Then Peter preached. I glanced around the church. I thought how little Peter's own people knew of the restrictions under which he labored. The situation for the Hungarian church, I reflected, seemed hopeless.

Afterward when we talked with Peter, I voiced the concern weighing heavily on my heart. "Can't something be done to keep the church alive and growing?"

"Not in the 'official' church," Peter sighed. "The 'official' church is doomed. But no matter. It's only a screen anyway—something that lets the authorities think they are in control."

"And unofficially?" Mona asked.

"Unofficially," Peter smiled, "there is hope. Come. I'll show you the *real* church!"

We followed Peter to a home where about 120 people were packed into a small room. I looked around curiously. Most of them were under 30, I guessed, with only a few gray heads among them.

For the next two-and-a-half hours we watched a drama portraying the life of Elijah. Young people acted out the desperate spiritual and political conditions of Elijah's day. Elijah's feeling of aloneness. His desire to die. And God's reassurance that 7,000 others had not given in to evil. The overriding message of the play was the need to remain faithful to God, avoiding compromise at any cost.

I knew the play could become a blessing to a much larger audience. As it progressed, I kept busy with my slide camera, filling roll after roll of film in an effort to catch every scene. In following months, we typed the script and made many copies of the slides. We prepared an audio-visual rendition of the play and sent it all over the country, as well as into Hungarian-speaking areas of Romania and Czechoslovakia.

I take great satisfaction in knowing that that audio-visual presentation was not scripted in the United States or Western Europe. It is a product of Hungary, conceived and created by the dedicated youth of Peter's *true* church. I filled in where I was needed, enabling those young people to minister to the larger Body of Christ themselves. This is just one example of the way we westerners can support the Eastern European church as it widens its ministry.

XII
God's Heroes Behind Communist Lines

Fog blanketed the West German countryside as Tim and I approached the border of Czechoslovakia.

"Time for a car check," I said to Tim, my companion on that trip. I turned off the highway and parked the car on a secluded road. We set to work.

Our personal Bibles had to be hidden, and we combed the car for bits of paper or notes which customs officials might question. I knew foreigners traveling in Eastern Europe were not subject to the torture the residents sometimes experienced. But the least suspicion that we were missionaries could lead to lengthy interrogation or even a prison sentence on a trumped-up charge.

Satisfied that everything was in order, we got back into the car and bowed our heads to pray. "Lord, blind the guards' eyes to anything which would make them suspicious," we prayed. "Take us safely into Czechoslovakia to minister to your people there."

We continued on our way. Thirty minutes later we joined a line of cars waiting for the signal to proceed to the Czech border station across the ravine. Czech guards, armed with machine guns, patrolled their borders. Finally one of them waved us ahead and we crossed the ravine.

"They'll check our documents first," I told Tim as we parked outside the station. "Then the car."

A guard took our passports, and the now familiar waiting routine began. But it was not to be for long. Within 20 minutes a guard returned our passports to us.

"Open up," he said sullenly, jerking his head toward the car. I opened the trunk, and he poked about with much apparent interest. "Okay," he grunted. "Close it up."

I closed the trunk and Tim and I got back into the car. "That was easy," I said as we pulled away. "It often takes hours, and sometimes they are very thorough."

We waited in another line of cars before the huge iron gate through which we would actually enter Czechoslovakia.

"No vehicle could run that gate!" Tim exclaimed, gazing at the huge cement pillars into which it was set. "Each of those pillars is as big as a car!"

"It was also built to keep Czechs and Slovaks from coming *this* way," I reminded Tim.

Soon the gate opened. We drove through, past guard towers, electric fences and a further checkpoint. Another mile or two and we reached the first of many villages which dot the countryside of Czechoslovakia.

"Look at all those hammer and sickle banners!" Tim exclaimed. "And those signs. What do they say?"

"I can't read Czech," I replied. "But the signs usually say such things as, 'In eternal alliance with the Soviet Union.' Or, '35 years of freedom.' Or, 'Friendship with the Soviet Union is the heartbeat of our country.' "

"Is it like this everywhere?" Tim wondered. "Constant propaganda?"

"It varies from country to country," I answered. "You'll see."

We drove on, finally arriving around noon in Plzen, a

large industrial town. Dull gray apartment buildings lined the streets, with hardly a tree or patch of grass to break the monotony. Then factories with smokestacks belching black and yellow clouds. We saw few pedestrians on the streets and even fewer cars.

I drove to the center of the city and parked in front of a hotel. "We'll eat lunch here," I said.

"This building looks abandoned," Tim said.

"I think it's open," I answered. And we walked past the smokey windows and in the front door. The second floor dining room was a huge dark room filled with people talking quietly or eating their lunch in silence.

We sat down and ordered our lunch, the same dish everyone else was having. Afterward, when the waiter brought our check, he bent down to pick up our empty plates.

"I would like to change money," he said very softly.

I looked at him to be sure I had heard correctly, but his face was impassive. He lingered over the table. "No," I said, realizing he was waiting for an answer. "We have nothing to change."

Back in the car, I explained to Tim. "We are only allowed to change money in official banks against a very poor exchange rate. That's why the government likes Western tourists. But Eastern Europeans like western currency," I said, "so they can buy blue jeans, cassette players or radios on the black market. Or they can go to special shops which sell western goods and accept only western currency." I paused for a moment, then added, "It could have been a trap too."

By late afternoon we reached Prague, a once glorious city of wide cobblestone streets and many statues. We headed directly for John Huss Square in the center of the city.

Crowds filled the square almost as if it were Sunday. On a balcony, high atop a belltower, a brass ensemble struck up a tune just as Tim and I got out of the car. We looked up at the musicians, shading our eyes against the afternoon sun.

The ensemble played a short tune then put their instruments down and leaned over the balcony railing to watch the people below. A few minutes later they picked up their instruments again and played another tune. Though no one applauded, people in the square seemed to enjoy the music. With the musicians so high above the crowd it almost seemed as if they lived in the tower, their only concern to play for the crowd below.

Embedded in a stone wall near the medieval city hall was a marvelous old clock with several small windows and doors surrounding it. As the huge minute hand crept toward the hour the crowd in the square turned expectantly to the clock. Tim and I joined them, wondering what the attraction might be.

Suddenly a bell chimed. The little windows and doors around the clock flew open. Intricate medieval carvings of the twelve apostles marched out through the little opening and paraded around the clock. Then finally they disappeared. The crowd watched in delight, and drifted slowly away.

Imre, Leader of Bible Study Groups

We spent a night in Prague, visiting various contacts. The next day we journeyed to other Western Czechoslovakian cities, ministering when and where we could. Finally we headed for the unspoiled countryside of village-speckled Eastern Czechoslovakia. In one of the larger villages a man named Imre had lived.

"Imre was so sick five months ago," I told Tim, "that I said good-bye to him then. I'm sure he's with the Lord by now, but his wife will tell us who we should talk to." And I went on to tell Tim about Imre, the key Catholic lay leader in one of Europe's most dynamic underground Bible study movements.

Imre had developed cancer. In its early stages he was treated in a hospital. But one day he was mysteriously discharged and deprived of further treatment: One of

Imre's nurses had come to know the Lord through his testimony; this was unacceptable to Communist authorities.

"Some of our teams took medicine to Imre after that," I said, "but he just kept getting worse.

"The Communists put him in jail once even while he was dying," I continued. "But they finally sent him home. They were afraid he would die in jail." I paused, then added softly, "He was only 30 years old."

At the edge of Imre's town, we parked our car and walked to the house where he had lived. When I knocked on the door, it opened a crack.

"I came to ask about Imre," I said.

Suddenly the door flew open wide and there stood Imre himself! With exclamations of mutual surprise and delight, we hugged each other warmly.

"How are you?" I asked when we were settled inside.

"Recently I've been better," Imre answered. "Many people are praying for me." But he seemed reserved. I waited for him to go on, sensing that he had some unhappy news to tell us.

"The police searched my house a few weeks after you were here," he said. "They didn't get any important information or quantities of literature. But they took all my books and every cassette I had, even the blank ones."

"A single cassette costs about four days of Imre's disability insurance," I explained to Tim.

"After the police took everything," Imre went on, "my wife became so upset. She took my little girl and left me."

I sat silent, not knowing what to say.

"She's living with another man," Imre finally finished, pain clouding his thin face.

"I'm sorry," I said softly, gripping his shoulder.

"Her faith was not strong," Imre said heavily. Then he brightened. "But the police didn't take my Bible! That and my faith are the most important things in the world to me."

I looked at Imre, feeling at the same moment both his loneliness and the strength of his faith. His words would return to me often in the next few weeks.

"We are printing 20,000 New Testaments right now," I told Imre later. "We're trusting God to supply the funds through western Christians who care. We'll bring them into Czechoslovakia late this summer."

"Oh, praise God!" Imre exclaimed. "I've been waiting for this for two years. Our young people are so hungry for the Word."

That evening Imre took us to one of the many cell groups he supervised. About 15 young adults, 30 years old and younger, were present. The main emphasis of the group was on prayer for revival and on Bible study geared to applying New Testament teachings to individual lives.

The Bible study movement in the Czech Catholic church is led by lay people. "But," one of the group members told us, "the number of born-again clergy is slowly growing!"

"Bring us evangelical teaching materials," another member begged. "And books like Billy Graham's *How to Be Born Again*."[22]

"But most importantly New Testaments!" added another.

During the meeting, the young people sang a hymn in their own language. The tune was familiar to us. Tim and I sang along in English:

It only takes a spark to get a fire going.
And soon all those around can warm up
    in its glowing . . .[23]

Later, while we walked back to Imre's house, I thought about the words of the song. The little group of youth who had sung it represented *seven million* Czechoslovakian Catholics. Their spark was beginning to spread through the underground Bible study movement. Soon millions of people would begin to feel the warmth.

"Now," Imre said later, in broken German, "I'm going to take you to someone who can translate for us. Then we can speak more freely." Imre spoke no English and little German. Communication among us had been laborious. I could see that he wanted to give us what might be a last message.

Tim and I left the house together almost immediately. Minutes later Imre joined us, and we cautiously followed his directions to a suburban home.

Imre led us inside and up a flight of stairs. The owner of the house pulled the drapes across the windows, shutting out any intruding eyes, as we sat down by the glow of a single lamp.

Imre talked, his face profiled by the lamp's soft glow. The pain of his cancer was obvious, but there was also joy on his face.

"I appreciate the Bibles and literature your teams bring," he began. "We have secretly duplicated Billy Graham's books and some of Andrew Murray's. But there are never enough, because the number of believers keeps growing constantly.

"There are at least 10 groups right now here in our town, and they all need literature and Bibles. I'll give you a name later of someone to whom you can deliver those 20,000 New Testaments when they are ready. I will probably not last until the end of summer.

"The situation keeps getting worse for us," Imre went on. "Communist pressure against Christians is increasing. Sometimes secret police even disguise themselves as westerners. They drive up in cars with western license plates, speak perfect English or German, give us money to help distribute Bibles, and generally act like believers. Then, after collecting evidence for a few months, they make arrests.

"They're making it more difficult in the schools too. In a meeting this year with some parents, one teacher talked about what a progressive educational system we have, free from backward religious teaching. Some of the parents stood up to her right then and there!

" 'We thought this was supposed to be a democratic country,' they said. 'If we want to give our children a religious education, that's our decision to make.' That had to take courage," Imre shook his head. "Those parents could be in for lots of police harassment.

"In the light of the youth movement in our cell groups," he continued, "some traditional Catholic parents are beginning to worry. They wonder what will become of the traditional church. For them, Christ and tradition are wrapped up together in one bundle.

"But we cannot lean on traditions. Jesus Christ and His word are all we can trust. That's why we need New Testaments so much. We want to get the truth from God's own Word and encourage a *personal* faith."

It was very late that night when we finally said good-bye to our interpreter and prepared to leave one at a time. In a few minutes Tim, Imre and I were together again in the car.

We didn't talk much on the way back to Imre's house. We were too tired to make the monumental effort required to communicate properly. Imre sat silently beside me in the front seat of the car. Finally he reached over and put his arm around my shoulders, giving me a hug. It was an emotion-packed moment. Tremendous Christian love hung, unspoken, between us.

A few blocks from Imre's house we stopped at a corner to let him out. I turned to him and he grabbed me and hugged me again, hanging on for a long moment. When he finally leaned back to look me in the eye, his own eyes were filled with tears.

"Good-bye," he said softly.

"Good-bye, Imre," I said, but he had already jumped out of the car. "I'll see you in heaven," I called softly after his departing figure.

In the following days we traveled through Czechoslovakia, meeting others and ministering as opportunity arose. But those last hours with Imre lingered long, just below the surface of my mind, flooding my thoughts at odd moments.

Anton the Bold

On another gray, windy day we crossed the border into Hungary. The countryside looked almost as depressing to me as the weather. We headed straight for a certain village in search of Anton, the pastor of a Hungarian Reformed Church.

Narrow dirt streets led us finally to Anton's open gate. I turned the car quickly into the courtyard. Tim jumped out and closed the gate against prying eyes.

Anton welcomed us at the door and led us laboriously into the house. He had no feet and only one leg, but helped by his prostheses, his handicap seemed hardly to slow him down!

During the afternoon we learned that Anton's favorite topic was his church, and especially the young people in it. About 14 youth ranging from 16 to 25 years of age meet regularly with Anton to pray, sing, and discuss Scripture passages they have read between meetings. They conclude by listing ways to apply specific Scriptures in their daily lives.

"We also work with children," Anton said, "25 or 30 of them. Most of our families are small, you see.

"The children usually accept Christ when they grow up. I send the young people to visit the children in their homes. They in turn invite the older children to youth meetings in order to witness to them."

"Can children attend church here?" Tim asked.

"Yes," Anton noded. "We have everyone come to church. We are not officially allowed, however, to work with youth and children separately. But I encourage it anyway."

"Are government officials aware of this?" I asked.

"I think so," he answered. "And they do try to harass and intimidate us from time to time. But I think their determination has worn down considerably over the years."

"How big is your church?" Tim wondered.

"We have 250 people. About half of them are definitely reborn people. The government allows me to hold only four meetings each week. That is just barely enough to give my people a good biblical basis for their faith. I use a combination of preaching and expository teaching. I invite questions from the congregation right in the meetings so I can deal with whatever concerns them."

"The government 'relegated' Anton to this little village because his ministry was too successful in the city church he once pastored," I explained to Tim.

Anton nodded. "I had five thriving services and a Bible study every Sunday. My bishop became fearful of government retaliation so he sent me here. Supposedly I can do less damage to church-state relations in this place," Anton laughed. "Our bishops are all hired by the State. Most of them capitulate to government pressure in order to hold their positions.

"I'm very much concerned about our pastors. Many of them are influenced by bishops who bend under the pressure of the State," Anton went on. "Part of my unofficial ministry right now is visiting such pastors all over this area to encourage them. They are like lost sheep, especially in Romania and Czechoslovakia. Yes, I cross into those countries too. Whenever I can get Bibles and study materials I distribute them wherever I go."

Later that afternoon Anton told us about his early life. Born in Czechoslovakia near the Russian border, he lost his mother when he was 15. Life was very difficult and he was looking for any opportunity that offered a change of circumstances. Before long a rather drastic opportunity presented itself. The Russian army swept through Czechoslovakia in 1944, driving the German army before it. Anton, then a teenager, joined the Russian army.

Seemingly fearless, he led charge after charge

against the German lines. He quickly won four medals for his courage.

"Before long, though, I was wounded," he said. "First I was hit in the ear, then in both legs. As a result I had to suffer these two amputations. I spent more than a year in Russian hospitals. After the war they sent me to a hospital in Miskolc, Hungary. While I was there my father came to see me.

"I had left home a bitter renegade. I wanted never to go back to my father. Nor did I want him to see how little was left of his once proud son. But he came into my room. Our eyes met and we could do nothing but cry together. It was a cleansing moment. I knew everything was right between us. That experience of my father's forgiveness helped me later to understand Jesus' story of the wayward son. And it prepared me to receive God's forgiveness as well."

Leaving the hospital minus both feet and one leg, Anton decided it was time to enter the university. His father wanted him to study finance so he could become a rich banker.

"But I was restless. I couldn't seem to find my niche in the Communist party, even though I became a committed atheist. Almost any position I cared to seek would have been open to me, for I had a good war record and spoke fluent Russian."

When Anton was 19 a friend from the university took him to a secret Christian youth conference one weekend. Anton spent most of the weekend laughing at the Christian young people. But, to his own amazement, by the end of the conference he was ready to yield his life to Christ.

Later he heard God's call to the ministry. Neither his father nor his professors understood. "You are a hero of communism," they protested.

"I must live for Jesus or I will die," he answered. Soon the authorities began to denounce him as a traitor.

I looked thoughtfully at Anton as he continued to talk. Now a mature man, he still was just as fearless as the young boy who had led assault after assault against the German lines.

"What is there in this world that I should fear?" Anton said, as if he had read my mind. "The authorities get so frustrated because they can't make me tremble. They don't know how to get at me.

"By now, many of them know me personally," he continued. "Some of them even come to me secretly with questions about the Christian faith. I've talked to them often, and I've given them Bibles!

"Sometimes, in turn, these individuals are good to me. They warn me when other authorities are about to clamp down on me. Through them, God takes care of me.

"And sometimes a guard will let something slip by, and I don't quite know why. Once I crossed the Hungarian-Romanian border with my car loaded down with Bibles and literature. A border guard discovered the Bibles. 'Why are you taking these across the border?' he asked.

"I replied, 'I am a war hero who now serves Jesus Christ. I have no choice but to do this. It is my Commander's orders!'

"The guard put his head back in the car and poked around some more. He uncovered all kinds of Bibles and literature. Finally he backed away. 'Close it up,' he said. Then he turned to another guard and said, 'I didn't find anything.'

"He obviously was sympathetic," Anton smiled. "Perhaps he was even a believer. Or could it be that, being a military man himself, he could understand my sense of being 'under special orders'?

"Once the Communists suspended my passport for three years. As if that would stop me!" he laughed. "My wife goes into Russia with the car full of literature too. So we kept right on smuggling!

"You know," he said, becoming thoughtful, "I believe there is a revival going on in Russia. No people on earth have a greater spiritual hunger than Russians. Everything is so controlled that it is hard to arrive at figures, but I think there are far more believers than we know."

Later we left Anton's house heading for Romania. How strikingly similar were Anton and Imre. Though they lived in different countries they had proven more than a match for the same kind of foe. The situation was virtually identical in every country we visited. Oppression had succeeded only in forcing the people to band together in underground movements or churches for the secret study of God's Word.

"The results of communism are amazingly uniform wherever in the world it has gained control," I said to Tim. "Likewise the effect the gospel has upon the hearts of men is strikingly similar no matter what their race or culture. You can recognize His people wherever you find them.

Imre, a Czech Catholic. Anton, a Hungarian Reformed pastor. Two of God's many heroes who live beyond what we call the Iron Curtain. Their faith is like that of the "cloud of witnesses" spoken of in Hebrews 12. Beholding their faithfulness under adversity, I was more inspired than ever to run the race God had set before *me*.

XIII
Hope for Romania

"Congratulations, Tim!" I said as we drove away from a border station bristling with electric fences and watch towers. "You are now in Romania!"

"Home of the legendary Count Dracula," Tim grinned.

"Count Dracula was supposed to be from a part of Romania called Transylvania," I said, "and guess where we are right now! In Transylvania!"

As we wound our way through one small village after another, I had the strange feeling that we were slipping gradually back in time to a simpler, more medieval era. Bonneted children played among faded cottages. Peasants, dressed in black, bent over their labor. Now and then we passed a rumbling horse-drawn wagon.

"What! No Communist banners or slogans?" Tim exclaimed.

"Not in Romania," I smiled. "Romania's ties with Russia are not that close. The government here sometimes even dares to defy Soviet policy."

"Is there greater freedom here then?"

"No. Romania is actually one of the more oppressed Communist countries."

Around noon we reached a sizable city. I selected a hotel from the tourist guidebook and we drove directly to it.

Tim looked curiously around the hotel lobby while I completed the details of registration. Once an elegant place with marble staircases and huge marble pillars, it now resembled an old brown-tone photograph. An ancient cage-elevator hung suspended between the first and second floors, and the whole scene suffered from poor maintenance.

Under cover of nightfall we made our way to the home of a Baptist family I had known a few years earlier. The next day they took us to meet the pastor of a large Baptist church. Later we traveled deeper into Transylvania and found a pastor whom I will call Alex.

Alex was built like a bulldog and his face shone with the kind of rugged goodness I imagine may have characterized Old Testament warriors like Caleb or Joshua. And just as Caleb and Joshua refused to back away from the challenge of conquering the Promised Land, so Alex delighted to accept the challenge of Communist oppression like a true soldier for God. The result? No device yet invented by Communists has been able to curtail Alex's influence. His ministry had become possibly one of the most successful in Eastern Europe.

Born and reared in Transylvania, Alex became a Christian at age 13. Before World War II he studied theology, but the war postponed his dream of becoming a pastor. His father had been a coal miner so Alex was compelled to help the Nazi war machine by working coal mines in Germany. The mines became the school God used to give Alex the strength he would need for spiritual battles later in life.

After the war, Alex returned home to see the Communist python already encoiled around his homeland. To combat the spreading blight of atheism Alex returned to his original desire and became a pastor. Thus began Alex's years of deadly cat-and-mouse games with the Communist regime.

"They've relocated me eight times because my churches have thrived so well," Alex told us. "They've also imprisoned me several times, and once they sent me back to the mines for six years."

All to no avail! As thoroughly unstifled Alex explained: "In fact, the authorities have helped me do the work of an apostle by moving me around so much!" he said, eyes asparkle. "They meant it for evil, but God used it for good.

"Finally, they moved me to this city," he continued. "Unable to curtail my influence by moving me from village to village they put me here in the church closest to their headquarters in order to watch me more closely. They apparently didn't stop to think that the people who live in this part of town are mainly brawny, toughened industrial workers—exactly the kind of people my years in the mines have best prepared me for. I understand them, and they know that I understand.

"Placing me here for punishment was like punishing a rabbit by throwing it into a bramble thicket! Or like punishing a pig by condemning it to a mudhole!

"Actually, though, the city is a harder place to work. The authorities are never far away, for one thing. Then, also, some city people think they are supposed to be more sophisticated and therefore less interested in religion. But my parish of brawny industrial workers is thriving."

"How do you get each church ready for the day you will be moved to the next one?" I asked.

"My main strategy," Alex replied, "is to practice the principle Paul taught Timothy. 'The things you have heard me say in the presence of many witnesses entrust to reliable men who will also be qualified to teach others' (2 Tim. 2:2).

"Thirty years ago at the beginning of my ministry I

began training laymen. I still do. By the time I have to leave a church, capable lay leaders are in charge in any case! Even if a liberal, loyal-to-the-state pastor succeeds me, the church has its own strength to carry on.

"Lay people, rather than the organized church structure, are the hope of the church anyway," he continued. "They are the living church."

"Then the real heart of the church is underground, isn't it?" Tim asked.

"That's right!" Alex agreed. "I have a circle of laymen right now whom I train and lead. I don't really ask them what they do with the training I give them, but I know they use it to lead smaller underground groups. Actually, what I pass on to these leaders reaches about 150 Bible studies and youth groups."

"Is most of your effective work underground then?" I asked.

"No, there is much above ground also," Alex answered. "A thousand people attend my church. We also hold youth conferences in which the auditorium is packed out with youth. The underground part of my ministry is focused on mini seminars and retreats which we hold in homes or out in the countryside for lay leaders."

"How have you managed to stay in this church," Tim wondered, "when you are doing so many things the authorities must dislike?"

Alex grinned. "I asked for a transfer," he said.

Tim and I glanced at each other, momentarily perplexed. Then suddenly we got the point. When Alex requests a transfer, the authorities think he is hoping to widen his ministry in some way. So they leave him right where he is, hoping to forestall whatever he has in mind!

"There are spies in every church," Alex told us sadly as we talked on. "They pray and sing and study right along with the flock, but they are quick to report our unauthorized activities to authorities."

Then Alex leaned across the table and looked at us with a very serious expression on his face. "You westerners cannot understand the situation we live under here," he said intensely, emphasizing every word. "You must be sure never to use my name or identify my church."

I nodded solemnly. "I understand."

In parting, Alex told us, "Ask the churches in the West to pray for us. Tell them not to weep for 'the poor suffering Eastern European Christians.' Rather, tell them to shout for joy! God is working! We are a Victorious Church! Some day the true church of Jesus Christ in Romania will witness to the whole world. You will come back, Hank, and speak openly in my church!"

The following Sunday was to be our last day in Romania. Tim and I had decided to spend it visiting churches. It was a beautiful bright morning and when we left the hotel it seemed the whole city had come out to enjoy the day.

First we went to a Pentecostal church, filled to the doors with an eager congregation. Neither Tim nor I could understand the Romanian language but the preacher's message sounded fiery. It was interspersed with periods of prayer in which the whole congregation knelt to join.

After about a half hour we decided to move on. Down the street we went into a Baptist church. It was filled with about 300 people, some of them standing in the aisles. I knew that in a later service so many people would crowd in that there would be no standing room left.

Tim and I stood near the door, watching. A young black African came in and we glanced at him. Smiling, he came over to us, holding out a welcoming hand. He spoke to us in English.

"I'm from Nigeria," he told us in response to our questions. "I'm in my second year of engineering. At home I go to a full gospel church, but here I found this church."

"How did you happen to come to Romania for your engineering degree?" I asked.

"I got a scholarship," he answered. "The government gives scholarships to many Third World people. There are actually quite a few African Christians studying here, but most of them avoid the church."

"They're probably afraid their education will be jeopardized," I commented to Tim later. "Communist governments provide these scholarships to create disciples who will take communism back to the Third World. I believe there are about 40,000 Arab students in Romania too."

When Tim and I left the Baptist church we headed across the bridge at the edge of town to a slum outside the city limits. "There's a Gypsy church over here," I told Tim. "Gypsies aren't allowed to live inside city limits, but there are 100,000 of them in Romania. Probably about 3,000 are Christians. A revival has been going on among them."

In the midst of the mud and squalor of the slum we found a shack of a church, filled with 500 colorfully clad people. We went inside and stood among them. We could feel their welcome immediately. I had visited the church before and I had been moved by the pleasure these despised people have in knowing someone cares enough to join them.

The congregation was singing indigenous music, accompanied in good Gypsy style by wailing violins and a thumping big bass fiddle. Later a lady got up to lead the congregation in a soft, sweet song of praise. Goose bumps popped out on my arms and I joined wordlessly in the spirit of praise. Could any western anthem outshine the beauty of this heartfelt Gypsy music?

"They'll overwhelm us with love and affection if we stay," I told Tim earlier. So we left before the service ended to avoid a prolonged farewell.

"I heard about a well-known Gypsy evangelist," I said to Tim as we walked back toward the city, "Yoan. The police beat him many times. They finally begged him to leave the country. He resisted at first but he finally gave in and emigrated."

We crossed a bridge and walked on to the center of the city.

"Look at that church," Tim said, pointing to a huge Romanian Orthodox church.

"Isn't it something! I've noticed it before," I said, stopping to gaze again at the beautifully tiled walls, towering turrets and marble columns.

"Let's see what's happening inside," Tim suggested.

"Fine! Maybe we'll find a dozen old ladies in there," I chuckled facetiously.

We walked up to the heavy carved doors and pulled one of them open. Stepping inside, we found the sanctuary filled with at least 1200 people! They stood quietly, drinking in every word of the sermon. We stood at the edge óf the crowd and I looked up at a marble balcony high above us. A red-hued ceiling soared even higher above that. At the far end of the sanctuary, near the altar, the priest stood giving the sermon.

I could not understand the sermon any better than others we had already heard that morning. I cannot say whether the priest delivered a true word from God or not. But he preached with spirit, and the audience hung on his every word.

We left the church at noon and went to a restaurant for lunch. Inside the restaurant we were recognized as foreigners and taken immediately to a nice table.

"Look," Tim said while we waited to be served, "there's a large section over there which seems more crowded than this section. It must be for the common people."

"You're right," I said, looking around. "See that red curtain over there? I gestured with my chin. "Whenever the waiter goes back there I get a glimpse of tables with flowers. That must be for Communist Party officials and wealthier people."

"We're in the second-class section," Tim concluded.

We took our time over lunch, and afterward we remained at the table while I wrote notes about our morning visits to churches. Later we went outside and walked along the street until we came to a park. The park and the street were full of people wandering along or sitting on benches, talking and enjoying one another and the lovely day. Occasionally a car passed on the street at the edge of the park.

"A lovely day, some free time and companionship are all they seem to need for entertainment," I remarked.

That night Tim and I went with an interpreter to visit in the home of a local Christian man. While we talked with him we asked about the Romanian Orthodox Church.

"I never expected to find the church *that* full," I said. "Are people really hearing the Word?"

"People are so hungry," the interpreter answered. "They go anywhere they can hear something. They will even gobble up dry rules and empty words."

"Then the priest was not likely preaching the Word this morning?" I asked.

"Perhaps. Perhaps not," the interpreter answered. "Often what the priest says is biblical, but there are no living examples to help people understand."

"There are few who can explain the truth," our host put in. "Here in Romania we are so hungry for the Word of God. You know, whenever anyone gets a Bible or study book he uses it at home and then passes it around to all the groups in the Lord's Army."

"The Lord's Army is the lay-led secret evangelical movement within the Romanian Orthodox Church," I explained to Tim.

"We need Bibles and study materials so much," our host continued. "For 300 members of study groups, here in this town there are only *three* Bibles."

Back in the hotel that night I thought about all the people we had visited since leaving West Germany a few weeks earlier. There were Imre, Anton, Alex and many others. They had shared some of the struggles of their daily lives, and I had every reason to believe things were as they said.

Then I thought about the crowded churches we had visited that morning, and the hunger for God which the numbers indicated. Those crowds, along with the dedicated men we met, give an accurate picture of the situation as it really is in Eastern Europe.

The Imres and the Antons, the people who put their lives on the line daily for Christ, are the future of the church in the East. The hunger for God is tremendous. There is hope! I believe there is special hope for Romania. For those who hunger and thirst after righteousness will be filled!

XIV
A World in Turmoil

The world is in turmoil, and that turmoil is not limited to faraway places. When I speak in the West, I hear growing concern about economic and moral decline and fear of a third world war.

The world climate today is ripe for Communist agitation in Asia, Africa, South and Central America, and also in Western Europe and North America. In 1980 the Kremlin issued a communiqué at the conclusion of a visit by French Communist Party boss, George Marchais. "The principal fact of the current world situation is the change in balance of forces," read the statement. "That is a powerful encouragement for the development of the class struggles in the world."[24]

The Real and the Counterfeit

In the church we sing "Faith of Our Fathers," referring to our Judeo-Christian fathers. However, Communists could also sing "Faith of Our Fathers," meaning the fathers of atheistic communism, such as Lenin and Marx.

We should not see communism as anything less than a faith. It is not merely a philosophy, but is a counterfeit religion. Atheism is an imitation which can survive only at the expense of religion. It is a parasite which benefits from all the social and moral concern, which religion has disseminated throughout the world, while denying the source of that social and moral concern.

A comparison of communism and Christianity reveals the following parallels:

Christianity	**Communism**
Primary motivating force: Love	*Primary motivating force:* Fear
Required commitment: Every thought in submission to Christ	*Required commitment:* Every thought conforming to the will of the Communist State
Unifying bond: Holy Spirit	*Unifying bond:* The spirit of Marxism/Leninism
Methodology: Evangelism	*Methodology:* Revolution
Goal: Christ's eternal kingdom	*Goal:* A world-embracing utopia under Communist control

Like Christianity, communism demands faith and total submission. Christianity offers the reward of eternal life, however, while communism, though it promises much, delivers little real reward.

The Battle Is Spiritual

The real foe, however, is not communism. If communism were to vanish from the earth today some other "ism" would take its place tomorrow. Our battle is not against a regime with soldiers, tanks and bombers. It is a spiritual battle against Satan and his realm. It will not be decided by armies, governments or diplomats but by prayerful evangelists, teachers and pastors—or the lack of them.

Our aim is not to kill or imprison men but to set people free spiritually, so that they may have life. We are called to extend God's kingdom in the midst of earthly kingdoms, not to overthrow earthly kingdoms by force. Only Christ Himself may apply force in that way. Our motivation is love, not hate. Though we do hate evil we love the ones whom evil has enslaved and compelled to serve its purpose, for they are blinded prisoners, as we ourselves once were. It is for love of such captives that we fight the battle. To win this battle we must take the offensive rather than merely defending ourselves against the enemy's tactics.

Our weapons then are spiritual. Three which we have occasion to use perhaps more often than any other are prayer, love and faith.

In my travels through Eastern Europe *I have often been made aware of the power of prayer.* Once on a trip into Poland border guards took me into an office while my companion, Jack, remained outside in the car. An official, scrutinizing my papers, began asking detailed questions about my car, my previous visits to Poland, my work and many related things. After about 20 minutes his questions became so probing that it was becoming difficult to conceal important information.

Outside in the car—although completely unaware of the touchy situation I was in—Jack became very concerned and began to pray fervently. Suddenly, back in the office, a loud knock on the door behind me interrupted my interrogator.

"Hurry it up!" an insistent voice called through the door. Distracted from his line of thought the officer quickly finished his interrogation and released me. I left the building with a sigh of relief, not even knowing whose timely interruption had delivered me. Jack and I entered Poland without further incident. Jack had prayed and the battle was won.

The Scriptures abound with examples of prayer used as a weapon. Prayer opened iron doors for Peter in Acts 12. King Herod imprisoned Peter but the early church prayed, and an angel of the Lord came into the prison and led Peter out.

When the Amalekites attacked Israel, Moses, supported by Aaron and Hur, lifted the "staff of God" in his hands, invoking God's help in Israel's struggle. By that act he reminded Israel of all that God had already done in response to Moses' upraised hands—at the Red Sea and in other crises. Meanwhile, down in the valley, Joshua and his army waged hand-to-hand combat. But the final outcome of the battle depended on Moses' prayers; for whenever he lowered his staff the Israelites began to lose. (See Exod. 17:8-15.)

We should notice the fact that it was Moses who became weary, not Joshua. Aaron and Hur had to hold up Moses' hands so that the battle could be fought to a victorious conclusion. There is nothing easier to extol the value of, but harder to be faithful in, than prayer.

When we from EEBM go into enemy territory we depend on the prayers of those who stay behind, those who perhaps cannot be involved in the actual hand-to-hand "combat" we experience. The final outcome of our work is dependent upon the prayers of our friends. I hope this book will be an encouragement to you to pray, to be like Moses, or like Aaron and Hur who held up Moses' hands. Together we may win the victory God wants to give us as we wait upon Him.

The second weapon is love. Where hate could only blind us, love opens our eyes to the need of mankind and causes us to reach out. Love's focus is always upon God and His grace, not upon ourselves or the enemy. If we look merely at the enemy we forget those who are his captives. But when we focus upon God we see people from His perspective, and love for them becomes possible. If any motivation other than love moves us we are doomed to stumble. We are unfit for battle.

The enemy tries to undermine our morale by mocking our faith. But with Jesus as our Commander there is no reason for fear or doubt. His power is more than sufficient. We can trust Him. If God is for us, who can be against us?

Like automatic doors which open only as we approach them, the doors God places before us open only as we approach them in faith. Even doors marked "closed to missionaries" open when God says "Go." We must be ready to respond in faith.

Obedience to the Commander

Obedience is the final question. Are we available to respond to God's call or must He find someone else to go in our place?

We cannot spend our lives as mere spectators. Personal involvement is imperative whether we "punch buttons" to send out long-range missiles through prayer or wield the "sword of the Spirit" in hand-to-hand combat on the front lines.

We dare not ignore the battle simply because our own well-being is not immediately threatened. For every time some distant battle is lost, the lines of battle shift closer to our own front doors. And we dare not allow fear to paralyze us. A friend of mine in Eastern Europe lived under the constant threat of arrest because Christian books were found in his house. At first, fear had gripped his heart, but later, living under constant government surveillance, he learned to see his problems from God's perspective.

"I know I could be arrested at any time but I'm not afraid anymore," he said. "I now see that it is worth giving *everything* for God. The price of my life is insignificant in comparison to the price Christ paid for all mankind!

"When I first became a Christian," he said, "I thought God would bless me with a trouble-free life. Now I know that He frees me to enjoy His blessings even in the midst of trouble. I am saved to live or die for God. Everything revolves around God, not me. With this perspective, I can learn to disregard the cost."

We too must run the Christian race regardless of the cost. We must discern not only the wickedness around us, but also the "cloud of witnesses" who throughout history have found God to be faithful and have been faithful to Him. Those witnesses are listed not only in the pages of the Bible but also in the pages of this book and thousands of other books as well; yet too few Christians today prepare themselves for a life of sacrifice by reading such testimonies.

As human beings we tend to seek the easy way. Otto, an East German youth worker, told a group of young people, "We like to look to the West for help and support, but God wants us to look to the East for opportunities to minister—yes, even within the Soviet Union itself. He has given us many helpers. Now we must become helpers to others. We must pass on to others what we have received from Him.

"Jonah," Otto went on to say, "is an example of someone who wanted to flee to the West—Tarshish, from his perspective. But his God-given task was in the East, in Nineveh, even though such a task was not Jonah's own natural choice."

In Otto's house hung a wall plaque which seemed to characterize his life: " 'Tis the set of our sails, and not the gales, which determines the way we go!"

Are your sails set to follow a divinely plotted course?

Or are you merely letting the gales sweep you on to who knows where?

What to Do If Threatened by Revolution

"First we will take over Eastern Europe," Lenin once said, "then the multitudes of Asia, and in the end we shall enclose the United States . . . the last fortress of capitalism."

Lenin urged Communists to spread what we now call "passivist thinking" in the West in order to weaken western resistance to the advance of communism. Thus he hoped that in the end a final showdown would not occur. The world would drop into Communist hands like an overripe fruit.

In many countries of the world today people are saying, "We never thought they would gain control here, but they did." True, some countries are more susceptible to Communist takeover than are others, and yet, unless proper safeguards are taken early, takeover is a possibility anywhere! Don't think it could never happen in your country. And if it does, remember that it will mean the loss of some of the church's freedoms, but it need not mean the end of the church! Readers of this book who live in lands susceptible to Communist takeover may profit from the following strategy, not merely for spiritual survival under communism but for actual triumph over it.

First, know the enemy's strategy. How much do we, in the West, know about communism's strategy? How many of our seminaries actively advocate world evangelism as a priority—including two-thirds of the world's population living in "restricted" countries? And how many are preparing Christians to flourish under persecution? How many Western church leaders have informed themselves about the suffering church in the East, let alone seek direct contact with that church? We must prepare ourselves by learning how Communists think and how Christians under Communist domination have learned to be a Victorious Church. Part of our strategy at EEBM is to help educate the Western church in such matters.

Second, you know your Commander so you can fight fearlessly. A Bulgarian Christian once said, "A man who is already wet doesn't fear the rain." Instead of seeking your own safety and security, seek first the kingdom of God and His righteousness. Saturated thus with an attitude of obedience to your Commander you will not have to worry about more "rain."

Be willing to take a stand, as Shadrach, Meshach and Abednego did when King Nebuchadnezzar ordered them to bow before his golden statue. They became, by Nebuchadnezzar's definition, lawbreakers—even though they knew the penalty was the fiery furnace. God did not deliver them *from* the fire; He delivered them *in* it. As a result their lives were not merely spared but they lost their bonds as well!

We must be willing to obey regardless of the consequence. The center of God's will is, after all, the only safe place in the universe. Let Him be Commander-in-Chief. And encourage believers around you to uphold the absolute standards set by Scripture. At the same time be willing to use creative methods to do God's work.

Memorize Scripture. Hide God's Word in your heart. If a hostile government ever confiscates your Bible you will treasure every word you have memorized.

Decentralize denominational structures. A Slovac priest said, "The strength of the hierarchy was the weakness of the church when Communists took over." Communists exploit hierarchies as ready-made devices for controlling the church. They will try to impose hierarchical structures even on churches which historically have rejected such structures.

The church must learn to function more as an organism and less as an organization. In a time of Communist domination, a national hierarchy will find itself under tremendous corporate and individual pressure from the government. In addition, government authorities will control any new appointments within the structure.

Develop lay leaders—tens of thousands of them. To do this, pastors must begin delegating greater responsibilities to lay leaders *now!* Provide training for them— on-the-job training. Take them with you on visitation. Teach them to pray, to teach, to disciple and counsel others.

Train each family to see itself as a cell-group, capable of growing, right where it is, should existing churches ever be closed by government decree. If congregations as we know them are forced to disband, any Christian family can become the nucleus from which a new church will grow, using the home basement or even a garage as a meeting place. Give families the training they need to fulfill such a role should the need arise. Large churches in South Korea, for example, are organized into tens of thousands of "cell groups," each of which can function as an isolated mini-church on a moment's notice. If ever Communists in North Korea should sweep down and impose themselves upon South Korea, Christians in South Korea are ready!

Secure duplicating and printing facilities. Plan ways to duplicate the Scriptures and study materials under difficult circumstances. These must be uncomplicated printing methods.

Keep a clear focus beyond yourself, and even beyond your own community. Otto, the East German who advised his young people to look to the needs of unbelievers and Christians in Russia, had the right idea. Looking beyond ourselves we see our own situation in better perspective. When we reach out to those in more difficult circumstances than our own it helps us to avoid self-pity.

Still, selfish love of pleasure and ease will, at least for a season, focus our attention upon ourselves as the center. There is no better cure for that than a little persecution. Daniel, the Czech intellectual who translates materials for EEBM, told me just before he was imprisoned: "Too much freedom leads to a loss of spiritual muscle, and too much persecution restricts activity. The best thing is to have a balance of both." Ivan, the pastor I met on my first trip to Russia with Frans, said that it is best to have a time of severe persecution, followed by a time of freedom, and then more persecution. Persecution purifies the church, then freedom gives it a chance to testify out of its renewed purity. Amazingly, Luke's Acts of the Apostles tells us that alternating seasons of persecution and freedom were exactly what God used to stimulate the witness of first-century Christians.

Our Response to the World

For many of us our only concern is for the security of our own immediate family, church, community and nation. While it is legitimate, and indeed necessary, to plan for such needs, a biblical perspective requires much more. Over and over again, from Genesis 12:3 to the book of Revelation, the Bible keeps using phrases like "all peoples" and "all nations." Sometimes it speaks of "every tribe and language and people and nation" (Rev. 5:9). Other times it uses the word "Gentiles" or "world." The Bible makes it very clear that God's plans include all such—not just ourselves. We must, then, become what are sometimes called "world Christians," i.e., Christians who live their daily lives with an all-people's perspective—keeping the center of their focus outside themselves and their own domicile.

Jesus said, "Whoever tries to keep his life [seek his own fulfillment] will lose it" (Luke 17:33). Exactly what, then, is an appropriate response to the whole world with all its peoples?

To begin with, Jesus told us to "go and make disciples of all nations, baptizing them . . . and teaching them to obey every thing I have commanded you" (Matt. 28:19,20).

Jesus' command has no boundaries. He did not send us into all the *free* world only, but into *all the world*. Jesus knew about hostile governments. That's the very reason He continued by saying: "All authority in heaven and on earth has been given to *me*" (Matt. 28:18, italics added). And when He commissions us, He encourages us with His presence: "And surely I will be with you always, to the very end of the age" (v. 20).

The battle rages all around us; the world is in turmoil. But there is a radical world-changing answer. The only question is, Are we willing to be a part of the answer? Are we ready to go into *all* the world?

Together, you and I can make a difference. But the commitment required of us is total. It's like the commitment of Alexander, a key leader in the growing unregistered home Bible study movement in Czechoslovakia. Alexander is a 60-year-old lawyer. God uses him to reach intellectuals and students for Christ.

One day when I went to Alexander's house, he turned his radio on before he opened his door to welcome me. He even held his radio in his hand while we talked, to mask our conversation. "My house has just been searched for a second time," he told me. "I think it is bugged now. I have been under constant surveillance for several weeks. There were four to six policemen stationed around to watch the house. One day downtown I saw 20 different secret police following me at different times all day long."

"You have already spent eight years in prison. What do you think they will do to you this time?" I asked.

Alexander looked down in silence for a moment, then he looked up at me. "I hope they are only trying to intimidate me, to make me stop working with the secret lay-movement."

"What are you going to do?"

"I'll just have to be very careful," he answered. "I cannot stop and do nothing."

After I left Alexander I thought about his example of daring to serve Christ in spite of probable consequences to himself; and in spite of the fear which must trouble him, at least sometimes. I remembered someone in Holland saying that a hero is not a person who is unafraid. A hero is someone who knows what God wants him to do and does it *even though he is afraid*.

The Bible says, "Keep your lives free from the love of money and be content with what you have, because God has said, 'Never will I leave you; never will I forsake you.' So we say with confidence, 'The Lord is my helper; I will not be afraid. What can man do to me?' " (Heb. 13:5,6).

There is only one thing that is important. That is to know God's will and to obey Him in spite of intimidating circumstances. When Jesus took our sins upon Himself, He did not let men intimidate Him. He obeyed the will of God, going to the cross in death, even carrying our sins with Him.

In spite of economic and political instability, pressure at work or at home, let us apply the example of Alexander and of the many others we have met in these pages. Let us not be afraid of men and their schemes. Let us rather do the will of God, knowing certainly that He is our helper. If Jesus is indeed our Lord then He will be our helper.

Let us not forget that we are in this spiritual battle together. Because we in the West do not suffer does not mean we can live at ease. In the body of Christ, "If one part suffers, every part suffers with it" (1 Cor. 12:26). Paul tells us in Galatians 6:2, "Carry each other's burdens, and in this way you will fulfill the law of Christ." Let us use the spiritual weapons available to us, not merely to defend, but to attack.

God does not see heroes. He makes heroes. And you can be one of them.

Conclusion

When the Son of Man comes in His glory all the nations will be gathered before Him. Then He will say, among other things: "Come, you who are blessed by my Father. I was starving for the printed Word of God and you brought me a Bible, even at the risk of a heavy fine!

"I was thirsty for teaching, and you brought me study materials in my own language!

"I was a stranger in a land foreign to you, yet you journeyed from afar to share good news with me!

"I needed someone to arouse world opinion concerning my loss of religious freedom, and you made my story known to thousands!

"I was sometimes discouraged because of my oppressors, but when you told me of the great things God is accomplishing beyond my own horizons, I took heart and persevered.

"I was the prisoner of an arrogant totalitarian government, but you braved long interrogations, threats and fines to visit me!

"Then the righteous will answer him, 'Lord, when did we do these things for you?'

"The King will reply, 'I tell you the truth, whatever

you did for one of the least of these Eastern European brothers of mine, you did for me.' " (Based upon Matthew 25:31-40.)[25]

Besides being able to travel personally and minister to Christians in Eastern Europe, you can be involved through prayer and financial support. The bimonthly EEBM Focus newsletter, sent at your request, gives you specific prayer points and news of the current situation. Your financial support to Eastern European Bible Mission will provide the Bibles and training materials that Christians in the East are asking for.

Notes

1. "American Preaching: A Dying Art?" *Time*, Dec. 31, 1979. p. 66.

2. Francis Schaeffer, *How Should We Then Live?* (Old Tappan, NJ: Fleming H. Revell Co., 1976), p. 127.

3. "Party Organization and Atheist Education" 1975. Published in the Soviet Union.

4. Aleksandr Solzhenitsyn, *Communism: A Legacy of Terror*, (New York: Harper and Row, 1975 as quoted in Schaeffer), p. 126.

5. Schaeffer, p. 127.

6. Dan Fisher, *International Herald Tribune*.

7. Zhamya Yunosti, 6 September, 1979 (according to Keston News Service-27 September 1979, Keston, England).

8. Ibid.

9. Ibid.

10. Menachem Begin, *White Nights: The Story of a Prisoner in Russia* (New York: Harper and Row Publishers, Inc., 1979).

11. Vladimir I. Lenin, *Selected Works of Lenin* (New York: International Publishing Company, 1971).

12. *Tarsadalmi Szemle*-December, 1977, Hungary.

13. Aleksandr I. Solzhenitsyn

14. *20 + 10 Jahre Danach* by A. Hlinke (Stephanuns Edition Verlag. AG 7299 Seewis, 1978).

15. Josif Ton, *The Christian Manifesto* (Keston College) England, 1976.

16. Andrew Nagorski, "The View from Lithuania," *Newsweek*, August 3, 1981, p. 48.

17. *Manifesto of the Communist Party*, 1848, Karl Marx.

18. Fr. Dmitrii Dudko, *Our Hope*, (Crestwood, N.Y.: St. Vladimir's Seminary Press, 1977), p. 23.

19. *Glaube in der Zweite Welt*-Dec. 1977, Zöllikan. Zurich, Switzerland.

20. *Life of Faith* magazine, England, July, 1978.

21. Ibid.

22. Billy Graham, *How to Be Born Again* (Waco, TX: Word, Inc., 1979).

23. "Pass It On," by Kurt Kaiser. © Copyright by Lexicon Music Inc. All rights reserved.

24. Kremlin statement, 1980.

25. Unidentified quote seen in different publications but without source.